Praise For

THE EIGHT PARADOXES OF GREAT LEADERSHIP

"*The Eight Paradoxes of Great Leadership* is an insightful and practical guide for leaders who want to grow their impact and influence, and do so in an authentic and effective way. Tim Elmore's perspective on leadership is grounded in both his own experience from building a dynamic organization and closely observing a number of other outstanding leaders. I highly recommend this book."

—Tim Tassopoulos,
President and COO, Chick Fil A

"'We're not experiencing an era of change, but a change of era.' This is one of many powerful statements in this book about leading in a complex age. As you digest this content, your leadership will soar to a new level. God knows we need leaders who are courageous and willing to practice the paradoxes that make them uncommon."

—Anne Beiler,
Founder of Auntie Anne Pretzels, Author, Speaker

"Leadership is really, at its core, a paradox—or a set of paradoxes. Tim Elmore captures eight of these paradoxes in an engaging, entertaining, and enlightening read that is sure to both encourage and challenge you and your team. As our world begins the difficult task of emerging from a global pandemic, we are in urgent need of the great leadership that Tim describes here."

—Dave Katz,
President of Coca Cola Bottling Company Consolidated

"Who would have thought that leadership today requires that we balance apparent contradiction? But that's exactly what Tim Elmore suggests in this insightful book. If you apply the paradoxes in this book, it will transform your leadership."

—Gene Smith,
Director of Athletics, Vice President, Ohio State University

"So much has been written about leadership today, but often it simply fails to describe the confusing complexity of what it *really* takes to lead in ways that uplift others, transform outdated approaches, and guide individuals and entities to thrive. Addressing what's needed most—particularly all the paradoxes involved in becoming a truly great leader—Tim Elmore's book examines brand new ground, helping us balance the seemingly contradictory traits leaders need to embody. Tim's decades of hands-on experience growing leaders—from young adults to highly accomplished C-suite executives—gives him a powerful lens for teaching us how to balance confidence and humility, visibility and invisibility, personal interrelationships with collective connection, teaching while being the student, and finally, timeless integrity with immediacy and relevance. If you want to be a leader who leaves a positive legacy, don't miss this book."

—Kathy Caprino,
Forbes Journalist, Author and Life Coach

"Humility and confidence. Vision and blind spots. High standards and gracious forgiveness. Effective leaders stand out because they are able to juggle seemingly contradictory traits like these to lead their teams well. Tim Elmore tells us how. I recommend this book to anyone who wants to become a leader worth following."

—Andy Stanley,
Author, Communicator, Founder, North Point Ministries

"Today's workplace is different than it was in the past. Team members are more educated and expect more of leaders than they did when I started my career. The eight paradoxes in this book address these complexities and offer doable solutions for leaders today. This book is practical, insightful, and fun to read."

—Hector Padilla,
Executive Vice President of Outside Sales & Service, Home Depot

"*The Eight Paradoxes of Great Leadership* is a must-read for all leaders—whether they are beginning their careers or already leading organizations. At a time when employees yearn for leadership that embodies social and emotional intelligence, this book will help you think differently about what it means to be an impactful leader in today's workplace."

—Camye Mackey,
Chief People Officer, Diversity and Inclusion, Atlanta Hawks

"If you appreciate nuance, Tim Elmore in this book unpacks superb examples of brilliant paradoxical leadership and then leads you to clear applications. If you don't yet appreciate nuance, I recommend you start—start right here with *The Eight Paradoxes of Great Leadership.*"

—Bob Taylor,
Founder and President, Taylor Guitars

"This book unlocks the secrets that make effective leaders so successful. It explains how they balance traits that seem paradoxical, yet others want to follow them. This is a must-read for any leader who wants to flourish in today's complex marketplace."

—John C. Maxwell,
Bestselling Author, Founder of John Maxwell Company

"Over the years, our managers and coaches have noticed a change in our players. These changes require better leadership from all of us who call ourselves leaders. For quite a while, we've benefited from Tim Elmore and his insights into leading the next generation. These eight paradoxes are prime examples of what we need to do in order to succeed. I recommend this book highly."

—Dayton Moore,
General Manager, Kansas City Royals

INTRODUCING THE JOHN MAXWELL IMPRINT

PUBLISHING

The John Maxwell Imprint is a new leadership-focused division of HarperCollins Publishing that seeks to extend and expand the legacy of leadership expert Dr. John C. Maxwell. Dr. Maxwell has been identified as the #1 leader in business by the American Management Association® and the most influential leadership expert in the world by *Business Insider* and *Inc.* magazine. A recipient of the Horatio Alger Award, as well as the Mother Teresa Prize for Global Peace and Leadership from the Luminary Leadership Network, Dr. Maxwell speaks each year to Fortune 500 companies, presidents of nations, and many of the world's top business leaders.

The mission of the John Maxwell imprint is to discover and publish books that identify with John Maxwell's personal values and philosophy of leadership. The authors will be men and women of integrity in their personal, business, and spiritual lives, who have demonstrated a desire to add value to leaders who multiply that value to people, whether through their teaching, writing, or business acumen.

The EIGHT PARADOXES *of* GREAT LEADERSHIP

Embracing the Conflicting Demands of Today's Workplace

TIM ELMORE

HarperCollins Leadership
An Imprint of HarperCollins

Published by HarperCollins Leadership, an imprint of HarperCollins Focus LLC.

ISBN 978-1-4002-2831-7 (eBook)
ISBN 978-1-4002-2829-4 (HC)

Library of Congress Control Number: 2021943614

Printed in the United States of America

24 25 26 27 28 LBC 10 9 8 7 6

TABLE OF CONTENTS

FOREWORD BY JOHN C. MAXWELL

Legend has it that an ancient Chinese curse went like this: "May you live in interesting times."

It was a curse because life always feels easier in boring, predictable times. A similar Chinese expression goes, "Better to be a dog in times of tranquility than a human in times of chaos."

I think it's safe to say that we live in interesting times. Even chaotic times.

And that is the reason for this book. *The Eight Paradoxes of Great Leadership* is about the complexities of leading in interesting, even outlandish times, when those of us who supervise teams enjoy very little certainty. In 2020, the year COVID-19 broke out, more than one leader told me, "I feel like I made a year's worth of decisions in a month."

The word that leaders began using daily was *pivot.* Organizations had to adapt to the new normal. Retailers had to pivot because all of our shopping for a while was online. Zoom had to pivot because suddenly the whole world was meeting virtually. Life became both easier and harder at once. We learned we could do life differently, and likely we will never return completely to the way we lived prior to 2020.

While I have taught *timeless principles* of leadership and teamwork for more than thirty years, I believe there are *timely paradoxes* that are also needed in our day. In fact, especially in our day. This book examines eight of these paradoxes that effective leaders practice when facing volatile and uncertain seasons.

To illustrate how essential these paradoxes are, let me ask you some questions.

Have you ever observed a leader who was overconfident and wished they embodied a little more humility? Or vice versa, have you witnessed a very humble leader who couldn't motivate people to do anything and wished they had a little more confidence? Bingo. What was needed was a paradox: people need both confidence and humility from their leader.

Have you ever watched a leader who did too much, never empowering others to step up and take their place on a team? I bet you wished they would've stepped aside and become invisible so that others could realize their potential. On the other hand, do you know leaders who are never around, who never set an example, and wish they would model what they want their team to do? Once again, those leaders needed to practice a paradox: people need a leader to be both visible and invisible.

You get the idea.

There are apparent contradictory traits that great leaders display and by doing so attract the best people around them. I believe many leaders haven't spotted these paradoxes because they feel like oxymorons. Surely, they can't both exist, can they? Yet they must. Today's teams are made up of people with high expectations of their leaders, and managing teams is far more complex than it was when I began my career in 1969. One moment your people need you to be personal with them, and the next they need you to speak collectively, to the entire organization. One minute, they need you to set high standards for them to meet; the next, they need you to model gracious forgiveness when they fail. One minute they need you to be present; the next, they need you to get out of the way.

- You'll feel like an empathetic counselor and a motivational coach.

- You'll feel like a cheerleader and a chaplain.
- You'll feel like a model (who sets the example) and a magician (who disappears).

I spoke to Tim Elmore as he was writing this book and immediately got excited about it. I think he put his finger on a missing piece in so many leaders' careers. I told Tim I wanted this book to be a part of the John Maxwell Publishing line of books at Harper-Collins Leadership. It aligns with the principles I have taught and complements them well. I have known Tim for forty years. We met when he was still in college and very green. But I saw something in him that I wanted to cultivate, so I invited him to join my team as soon as he graduated. We served together for twenty years, and I watched him grow and improve as a leader each year.

This book is an outcome of his leadership and his observations on leadership. It will challenge you to grow your social and emotional intelligence. It will stretch you to be multidimensional. It will provide you with practical action steps to embody these paradoxes.

Since we live in interesting times, we might as well enjoy the journey.

Paradoxical Leadership in a Complex Age

I reminded myself of the story about Isaac Newton several times as I sat in quarantine last year. At twenty-two years old, young Isaac was sent home from Cambridge University during the Great Plague of London in 1665. It was their own version of "social distancing."

And that's when the magic happened.

Without his teachers to guide him, Newton flourished. The period he spent away was later referred to as his *annus mirabilis*, the "year of wonders."

First, he continued working on math problems that he'd begun at Cambridge University. Believe it or not, the papers he wrote became the genesis of calculus.

Second, he acquired some prisms and began experimenting with them in his room, even boring a hole in his shutters so only a small beam of light could shine through. From his explorations emerged his theories on optics.

Third, outside his window was an apple tree. Yes, the apple tree we've all heard about. While parts of the narrative are legend, his assistant confirmed much of it is true. While Newton sat under that tree, an apple fell, which launched his thinking. From this apple, Newton developed his theory of the law of gravity and the laws of motion.

Back in London, a fourth of the population would die of the plague during 1665–1666. It was one of many outbreaks during the four hundred years that the Black Death pandemic ravaged Europe.

But today, we've all benefited from that outbreak.

Isn't it amazing that during a *great interruption*, Newton transformed it into a *great introduction* to an entirely new world of math and science? It was when he left a magnificent institution of higher education that he learned more than he could have in class. It was when life was on hold that he made his best progress. Our world was morphed by his time alone during a pandemic.

What an irony.

What a paradox.

Today, we live in the shadow of another pandemic. Our world was already complicated before, but the aftershocks of COVID-19 have only increased the challenges. Over the first twenty years of this century, our world became on-demand and instant access, driven by a gig economy, with a 24/7 news cycle on broadcast and social media. The most accurate description for our times comes from the US Army War College. It is the acronym, VUCA:

- Volatile
- Uncertain
- Complex
- Ambiguous

Pope Francis put it this way: "We're not experiencing an era of change, but a change of era."

These volatile, uncertain, complex, and ambiguous times have led to many difficult challenges.

LEADING WHEN YOU'D RATHER BE LEAVING

Two decades into the twenty-first century, thousands of leaders left their jobs, decisions made by them or their boards. Consider this. More than one thousand CEOs stepped down during the first three quarters of 2019, according to a report by the staffing firm Challenger, Gray & Christmas.[1]

Departures in the first nine months of 2019 exceeded the number of CEOs who stepped down during the first three quarters of 2008, which was the height of the Great Recession. It was the highest CEO turnover in that time frame, since the firm began tracking departures in 2002.[2]

By late 2019, more CEOs of major brands had stepped down, including eBay, Nissan, WeWork, and JUUL. The complexities of leading major corporations, pleasing stakeholders, and negotiating disputes with board members simply became too much for these executives. Furthermore, consider this. While Americans were distracted by the coronavirus pandemic, many CEOs stepped down in the first quarter of 2020.

- The CEO of Disney stepped down.
- The CEO of Hulu stepped down.
- The CEO of IBM stepped down.
- The CEO of LinkedIn stepped down.
- The CEO of Uber Eats stepped down.
- The co-CEO of Salesforce and Vlocity stepped down.
- The CEO of MGM stepped down.
- The CEO of Lockheed Martin stepped down.
- The CEO of Nestlé stepped down.

- The CEO of Volkswagen stepped down.
- The CEO of Mastercard stepped down.
- The CEO of T Mobile stepped down.
- The CEO of Harley-Davidson stepped down.
- The CEO of Victoria Secret and Bed, Bath, and Beyond stepped down.

Fortune magazine called it "The Great CEO Exodus of 2020."[3] Not all of these exits were sparked by COVID-19, but the weight of leading in such times is causing many leaders to wonder if it's worth it to stay. Whatever the patterns or conspiracy theories people find, one thing is sure: leading today is different than it was when I began my career. Our culture is anxious, and the marketplace is plagued by:

- A rapid rate of change, even fundamental change.
- Complicated circumstances with multiple stakeholders.
- An ever-critical public eye that spots and posts every flaw.
- A virus that becomes a pandemic and shuts everything down.
- A more educated team member who feels empowered by data.
- Convoluted and nuanced interactions that are scrutinized constantly.
- A fear of failing and an anxiety about the judgments of others around us.

Too often, organizations settle for leaders who do nothing, ensuring that at least they do nothing wrong. They choose *absenteeism* over *adversarial relationships.*

Consider a story I recently read about the dean of a reputable law school. "Two senior, well-regarded faculty members called the provost to complain about their dean because, they said, *he wouldn't do anything.* The provost responded by saying that he had a dean who was a drunk, a dean who was accused of sexual harassment, and a dean who was accused of misusing funds, but the law school dean never caused him any problems. So, the provost said, the faculty members would just have to deal with their dean."[4]

Do you see the logic behind the provost's argument? While a passive, even incompetent leader in the law school was suboptimal, he was the lesser of two evils. It was certainly better than active misconduct seen in the other college deans.

As far as I'm concerned, we play defense too often. And for that matter, we fail to play offense often enough. We tell ourselves that ours is a complicated day to be living in and become satisfied with avoiding losses. Or we settle for some form of leadership style or protocol that worked in the past. After all, what more could we expect? The top three candidates running for US president in 2020 were white males over seventy years old—Bernie Sanders, Joe Biden, and Donald Trump. Younger, more vibrant candidates either dropped out due to un-electability or were overwhelmed before the race began. Frequently, this is a picture of our world today.

I wonder how many times we have settled for average, even absentee, leadership just because we were used to it.

CONSIDER OUR COMPLEX WORLD

President Harry Truman once said, "Men make history, and not the other way around. In periods where there is no leadership, society stands still. Progress occurs when courageous, skillful leaders seize the opportunity to change things for the better."

I have reflected on this statement by Harry S. Truman for years. While I agree fundamentally with Truman, I also believe that these assertions are not mutually exclusive. *Leaders make history, but history also makes leaders.* There are situations that seem to draw out some marvelous gifts in leaders; that force them to be sufficient for those situations, capable of climbing to a new level with a team of people. The times they live in seem to beckon their potential. It is only when great leaders prove themselves by living up to the challenges that we recognize the history they have made.

We may just be in such times once again.

Reflect with me on the first two decades of the twenty-first century. History pivoted as our world moved into a new millennium. Those of us who felt our world had already become complicated found it becoming even more complex as the final chapter of the 1990s concluded and we entered the year 2000. Walk with me down memory lane.

- We began with the Y2K bug. This was a computer flaw that revealed just how vulnerable people are to apocalyptic fears.
- Next, we saw the dot-com era bubble burst. The financial downturn resulted in thousands losing jobs, money, and market share as companies went belly-up.
- Then, we endured a terrorist attack on September 11, 2001, sending us into an economic spiral, with companies and nonprofits going out of business.
- Soon, we witnessed a swelling number of scandals among large corporations such as Enron, Tyco, and Worldcom, which created a national suspicion of corporate corruption.
- Later came the introduction of the smartphone. In time we saw the addictive nature of these devices and the anxiety they foster. (It has been said: "When our phones had leashes, we were free. Now our phones are free, and we have leashes.")

- With the smartphone, we experienced the ubiquitous presence of social media. On these platforms surfaced stalkers, predators, and organizations tracking our activity.
- The Great Recession of 2008–2009 revealed how few had prepared for a financial downturn. The crisis led to mortgage foreclosures worldwide and caused millions of people to lose their life savings, jobs, and homes.
- Over the last decade, protests over racial equality, police brutality, gay marriage rights, gun control issues, women's rights, and sexual assault took center stage.
- The normalization of student loans became headline news as college tuition debt grew larger than credit card debt in the United States. Forty-two million Americans carry part of that load.
- Next, we saw an increase in mass shootings in America. In 2019, there were more mass shootings in the United States than days in the year (419).
- In time, we witnessed the normalization of addictions. From vaping to video games to pornography to social media to opioids and other prescription drugs, we found people used such coping mechanisms to endure their pain, angst, and depression.
- Political polarization was fostered by an electorate divided over the first minority president in Barack Obama and the first outsider president in Donald Trump.
- COVID-19 sent all of us home from work and school for months. By the end of 2020, almost 83 million people were infected and over 1.8 million died around the world. A record 6.6 million

Americans applied for unemployment in one week. It was a time of deep loss and poverty as people attempted to recover from the global outbreak.

- Finally, mental health issues reached epic proportions among Americans, especially young people. Anxiety is the most common mental health disorder in the United States.

Poor mental health is the unpaid bill of the twenty-first century. It affects nearly one-third of both adolescents and adults, according to the National Institute of Mental Health. The CDC reported that one in four young adults (ages eighteen to twenty-four) had contemplated suicide during August 2020, due to the pandemic.[5]

By the end of 2020, no one questioned whether we'd be talking about the COVID-19 pandemic for generations. The chief debate is—what do we compare it to? The Great Depression? The Spanish influenza? The 2008 financial crisis? September 11, 2001? World War II?

Is it any wonder that healthy leadership has become such a sought-after skill set? It is uncommon.

Over the course of my lifetime, the art of leadership has become convoluted. While our world has endured difficult eras in the past, including pandemics, world wars, famine, and the like, the times in which we live have shifted from *complicated* to *complex*. Rick Nason explains the shift in his book *It's Not Complicated: The Art and Science of Complexity in Business*:[6]

1. "Complicated" means a difficult situation stares you in the face. A student looking at a chalkboard, trying to solve a math problem in class, may find it complicated. Imagine that student decides to doze off and take a nap for thirty minutes. When the student wakes up, the problem will still be there, but it will be unchanged. Same problem, same

rules, a half hour later. No harder, no easier to solve.

2. "Complex" means a difficult situation stares you in the face that is constantly evolving. An air traffic controller at a commercial airport, helping planes take off and land, faces a tough challenge that doesn't stay the same. If she wakes up after a thirty-minute nap in the air tower, problems have gotten worse. What was complicated a half hour ago is now complex. Dynamics and nuances are shifting. Much tougher situation to solve.

Against this backdrop, you and I must lead people.

I chuckled at the story of a police academy on its final day of examinations. The officer proctoring the exam described an overwhelming scenario to his class of trainees—complete with a bank robbery, a fire hydrant spraying water everywhere, a person being mugged, a wild car chase, and people screaming as they ran in every direction. It was nothing short of a crisis. Each cadet was to offer what he or she felt would be their response to this horrifying situation.

The most honest answer came from the back of the room. One young trainee stood up and replied: "Remove uniform. Mingle with crowd."

This is an option we can't afford.

WHAT THIS BOOK IS ABOUT

Leading in the twenty-first century is, indeed, more complex than it was in past centuries. Leadership is seldom easy, but today it affords us the challenge of collaborating with a more educated, more entitled, more savvy population that has greater expectations of satisfaction and rewards than in past generations. Uncommon leaders stand out because they are able to juggle seemingly contradictory traits to lead such people. They balance paradoxes that make them worth following. Their paradoxical qualities are conspicuous as they require not just intelligence but the differentiating qualities of emotional intelligence, social intelligence, and moral intelligence. In the words of Adam Saenz, they are street smart, book smart, and heart smart.[7] Consider the following realities.

When people join a team today, they bring with them a higher level of:

1. **Education.** It's no secret that each new generation enjoys more formal education than previous generations. Today's young adults are much better educated than their grandparents, as the share of young adults with a bachelor's degree or higher has steadily climbed since 1968. "Among Millennials, around four-in-ten (39 percent) of those ages 25 to 37 have a bachelor's degree or higher, compared with just 15 percent of the Silent Generation, roughly a quarter of Baby Boomers and about three-in-ten Gen Xers (29 percent) when they were the same age."[8] To be clear, formal education does not equate to smarts but it does equate to an increase in what they expect and assume to be true in their leaders. One reason a leader's style in the 1950s could be more "top down" was fewer people were educated. Folks were more willing to simply be told what to do. Today, not so much.
2. **Entitlement.** A sense of entitlement is defined as "an unrealistic, unmerited, or inappropriate expectation of favorable conditions and favorable treatment at the hands of others." *Psychology Today* reports some examples of entitlement

include a disregard of rules, freeloading, and creating inconveniences to others. It's a form of narcissism causing people to believe they are superior to others; they can be disappointed easily and can feel more deserving of certain perks. Research has discovered that a growing number of people—especially young people—are developing an entitlement complex.[9] Studies on entitlement by the University of Hampshire found that youth scored 25 percent higher than people aged forty to sixty and 50 percent higher than those over that age range.

3. **Exposure.** Thanks to both media and social media, people joining our teams having been exposed to more content and realities than previous generations. A person (even a teenager) who has a smartphone is exposed to ten thousand messages a day, when you consider posts, ads, TV shows, emails, videos, signs, and conversations in person.[10] This exposure cultivates demands in the minds of team members—they've seen more so they assume they know more. And often they do. Our savvy population, however, has made us less forgiving. Consider the demise of George Washington's hero status of late, because we've discovered the less than heroic realities of his personal life. Savviness usually fosters cynicism and skepticism. May I say the obvious? The more cynical the team member, the more challenging they are to lead.
4. **Emotion.** It is ironic that in a culture with higher levels of education, which, one might assume promotes rationality and logic, we experience extreme expressions of emotion. We see a rise in emotional outbursts, outrage on social

media, political polarization, an unwillingness to compromise, and a rising inability in people to manage their emotions. Instead of objective research, more seek "confirmation bias." We're better at reacting than reflecting. Perhaps social media did this to us, but millions today are cognitively advanced, yet socially and emotionally behind. Drama has increased rather than decreased and we've been conditioned to crave it. ("Trash TV" is created to elicit emotion.) Our inability to navigate emotions like anxiety, to navigate conflict at work, and our failure to manage jealousy all reveal our need for a new kind of leader.

5. **Expectation.** In general, people today bring with them increased expectations about what they will experience at work. Keep in mind, expectation and entitlement are "second cousins" but they are not "twins." Entitlement is all about feeling we deserve something, a perk or an experience that is better than average. Expectations simply concern what we presume will happen. One is more about emotions, the other more about thoughts. Both can lead to powerful assumptions that leaders must deal with. Every leader today must understand that the expectations people have of leaders and jobs are on the rise and that conflict is created by the distance between expectations and reality.

Uncommon leaders differentiate themselves because they rise to these challenges. They display the ability to read and then respond to the nuances in a team member's language, allowing everyone to feel they belong and contribute. They live in the tension of two opposing views, weighing all possibilities, even when ruthless people demand they take sides or choose an extreme point of view. Uncommon leaders recognize most of life is lived with such tensions. Sadly, most people do not manage their emotions well enough to join them. It's why they need uncommon leaders. People are hungry for them.

Sadly, these leaders are rare because of the complex times in which we live.

Author David Rock writes, "The new generations coming into management positions have different needs from their predecessors. These people expect more from an organization. They want to develop personally; they value freedom and independence. They enjoy diversity and change. These people need a different type of leader than our command and control cultures have been churning out. They need leaders who help them shine, who help them fulfill their potential at work. Leaders who improve their thinking."[11]

Consider this truth: your influence expands based upon providing the scarcest resource.

Now that information is a commodity, available anywhere upon a search, informed leaders are no longer rare. What is rare is a leader who is socially and emotionally intelligent and who practices the paradoxes we'll discuss in this book with their teams. They bring a stunning form of insight into complex situations and find ways to achieve their goals. They're what past generations called "wise leaders." These leaders are essential today because people are drowning in information and yet starving for wisdom.

THE SECRET SAUCE IS SOCIAL AND EMOTIONAL LITERACY

Most of these paradoxes are about our emotional intelligence, not our cognitive intelligence. It's an issue of EQ, not IQ. For years, predicting effective leaders was a mystery to those who studied it.

Most felt it was merely an issue of *strong personality* and *high intelligence.* Over time, however, we discovered the issue was far more complex than this. The smartest people in the room didn't always make the best leaders. Consider how many times you've said:

How could such a smart person do such a ________ thing?

You fill in the blank: irrational, illogical, dumb, stupid, and so on. There is nothing more common than high-potential people who allow their emotional deficits to sabotage their careers. This is at least part of the reason we hear the cliché, *The straight A students will work for their C student peers one day.* Why? The C students had to make up for lower intelligence by learning to read social and emotional cues, while the smart kids relied merely on their intellect.

Travis Bradberry and Jean Greaves explain, "When emotional intelligence was first discovered, it served as the missing link in a peculiar finding: people with the highest levels of intelligence (IQ) outperform those with average IQ just 20 percent of the time, while people with average IQs outperform those with high IQs 70 percent of the time. This anomaly threw a massive monkey wrench into what many people had always assumed was the source of success—IQ. Scientists realized there must be another variable that explained success above and beyond one's IQ, and years of research and countless studies pointed to emotional intelligence as the critical factor."[12]

Social and emotional intelligence is "your ability to recognize and understand emotions in yourself and others, and your ability to use this awareness to manage your behavior and relationships."[13] The good news is that while IQ doesn't change much over our lifetime, EQ can be developed. We learn how to obtain and memorize information in school, but rarely are taught how to manage emotions and social cues. We enter our careers knowing how to read and report on the knowledge we've consumed but too often lack the skills to manage our emotions in the heat of the challenging problems we face. I often tell university students: *Success in school is 75 percent IQ and 25 percent EQ. In your career, it will be the opposite.*

The Emotional Intelligence Appraisal is the largest assessment of EQ in the world. Developed by TalentSmart, it has been taken by more than half a million respondents. The results are nothing less than astonishing. Over 90 percent of high performers are also high in emotional intelligence.[14] Coincidence? I don't think so.

Here's what's happening inside a leader's brain every day.

Every message your brain receives—everything you hear, see, smell, taste, and touch—comes via your spinal cord. Electronic signals are sent from that spinal cord and must pass through your limbic system (where you feel) on their way to the frontal lobe (where you reason). As you can see in the diagram below, the part of the brain where your emotions reside lies in the middle of the road as messages travel to where rational thinking happens. Further, the prefrontal cortex (the frontal lobe) is the last area to develop as your brain matures. The prefrontal cortex is typically undeveloped in teens, for example, which can manifest in extremely dramatic, emotional, and even irrational behavior. The area where they calculate consequences for actions isn't fully developed.

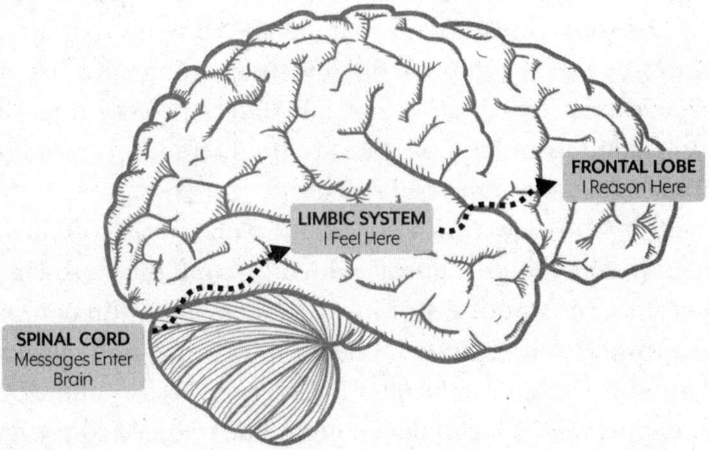

Although we are the most educated population in human history, we missed something in the education process: *training ourselves to manage our emotions.* We focused on academic or cognitive development at the expense of our emotional intelligence. We've filled our brains with reasonable content for our frontal lobe to store, but many of our interactions never make it past our limbic system.

There might just be an elephant in the room.

NYU leadership ethics professor Jonathan Haidt calls this phenomenon "the elephant and the rider."[15] He says that inside every one of us is a "rider" (our conscious, rational mind) sitting atop an "elephant" (our subconscious mind). That rider is much smaller than the elephant and often the elephant goes wherever it wants to, as the rider pretends to be in charge. When we feel strongly about something and emote—all the while rationalizing our emotional response—we have handed the reins to the elephant. We become brilliant justifiers of what we've blurted out, even when it's illogical to listeners. The issue we're debating isn't really the issue.

When Jack Welch was asked in an interview what the biggest mistake of his career was, he instantly replied, "Buying an investment bank." When questioned why, he said, "Because I didn't understand the culture." So often, a company is bought out and the CEOs assume the transaction is merely "complicated." In reality, the situation is complex, filled with colliding egos between managers, nuances in interactions, and different personalities and cultures that must blend. People are fluid and unpredictable—and that's good news and bad news.

In 1968, the New York Central and Pennsylvania Railroads merged to form Penn Central, which became the sixth-largest corporation in America. But just two years later, the company shocked Wall Street by filing for bankruptcy protection, making it the largest corporate bankruptcy in American history at the time. What happened? The problem couldn't be reduced to plugging in an algorithm and making a transaction. The leaders assumed it was merely complicated.

Managing people is a complex challenge. So is integrating two companies or figuring out how the market will react to a new product or strategy. Maybe you'll get lucky and figure it out once, but whatever you do the next time may not generate the same result.

Paradoxes are one answer to the complex challenges we face.

WHAT IS A PARADOXICAL LEADER?

As I spoke with one CEO recently, he grieved: *I must be a strategist, a cheerleader, a storyteller, a therapist, a futurist, and a motivational speaker.* Indeed, he may be right. I believe embracing these types of paradoxes may be our only saving grace in such complex times.

Defined simply, a paradox is an apparently incongruous or absurd proposition that, when investigated or explained, may prove to be well founded and true. And because the two parts of a paradox seem contradictory, we often fail to see the truth in them. How can these two opposing realities coexist? Only after careful examination does it make sense. Let me illustrate.

Countries and US states with higher happiness levels tend to have higher suicide rates, according to research led by Mary C. Daly of the Federal Reserve Bank of San Francisco.

This appears paradoxical until you consider that someone who is thinking of suicide may be even more vulnerable if they look around and everyone else appears extremely happy.

It's a paradox yet it's true.

While we were quarantined during the COVID-19 pandemic, the volume of road traffic declined measurably in Atlanta, where I live, yet traffic accidents rose. How could fewer cars lead to more accidents? It's ironic until you consider that because there were fewer automobiles on the road, people tended to drive faster and more recklessly, leading to more crashes.

It's a paradox yet it's true.

Paradoxes are strange, and yet, I believe they explain the unexplainable in effective leaders. Because our world today includes so many complex angles, only leaders who can serve in a multidimensional fashion have any hope of thriving in such volatile times. Embodying paradox has long separated exceptional people from average ones. F. Scott Fitzgerald once wrote, "The test of first-rate intelligence is the ability to hold two opposed ideas in mind at the same time, and still retain the ability to function."

Over the course of this book, I'll lead a reflection on some of the most important paradoxes essential for leading brilliantly during this third decade of the twenty-first century. To guide leaders in addressing these heightened expectations, this book explores and illustrates eight surprising paradoxes that effective leaders must practice as they lead. Embodying them enables us to stand out as extraordinary because:

1. Great leaders balance confidence and humility.
2. Great leaders leverage their vision and their blind spots.
3. Great leaders embrace visibility and invisibility.
4. Great leaders are stubborn and open-minded.
5. Great leaders are deeply personal and inherently collective.
6. Great leaders are both teachers and learners.
7. Great leaders model high standards and gracious forgiveness.
8. Great leaders are timely and timeless.

As you examine the chapter topics above, you'll quickly recognize that most of what differentiates uncommon leaders is their ability to read a situation before they lead a situation. They manage their emotions, observe their people, and choose the wisest response to reach their goal. They *adapt to adversity* and continue chasing their goal rather than merely *adopting adversity* as their dictator. In doing so, they embrace the necessary paradoxes along the way.

I began this chapter with the story of Isaac Newton, a college student who turned a pandemic into a "year of wonders." He created calculus, developed his theories on optics, and discovered the laws of gravity and motion. None of this may have happened had he not endured an interruption in his normal, busy routines at school, where professors directed his studies. Everyone benefited, including young Isaac Newton. He returned to Cambridge in 1667, with his theories in hand. Within six months, he was made a fellow. Two years later, he became a professor. Not bad for a twentysomething.

The concept is so simple, it eludes us. It was because Isaac Newton couldn't stay busy with his routine work that he made some of his most important discoveries. His *break* became a *breakthrough.* As I said, his *interruption* became an *introduction* to new discoveries. He chose to make his problem a possibility; to make his obstacles opportunities. When he chose to invest his time, not waste it, the stumbling block to his education . . . became a stepping-stone for growth.

So, how was this paradox created?

It appears Newton didn't see the plague as an interruption. He welcomed the change and leveraged being kicked off campus to learn in new ways. He took advantage of his solitude to muse and to create. Today, I think most people run from solitude. We are conditioned to put our earplugs in and fill our heads with noise. Turn the radio on. Drown out the boredom. While there's nothing wrong with this—it frequently prevents original thinking. Neuroscientists tell us that it's during times of boredom that our brains develop empathy and creativity. Fortunately, Isaac Newton had no video games or television with which to squander time. When nothing and no one consumed his time—he had time to reflect, imagine, and change the world.

Today, I think it's our best option in this complex world.

PARADOX 1

Uncommon Leaders Balance Both Confidence and Humility

Michael Dammann Eisner served as the chairman and CEO of the Walt Disney Company for more than twenty years, from 1984 to 2005. Under his leadership, the Disney brand was reawakened. From animated films like *The Little Mermaid* (1989) to commercial acquisitions like Miramax Films, ABC, and ESPN, Michael Eisner led with confidence.

It was during this time, however, that Disney also accrued a reputation for being tough negotiators and even tougher business partners. Their power was expanding, and they knew it. Eisner gained a reputation for hiring and firing people abruptly, for being unpredictable, and for going to court over issues that could have been resolved easily with less ego. Over time, Eisner became increasingly isolated and overbearing, which ultimately led to a shareholder revolt and his own dismissal. His final years, many say, were marked by self-destructive behavior, arrogant attitudes, and unnecessary emotion-driven public battles.

Enter Robert "Bob."

Bob Iger is a very different sort of leader than Eisner. He was a Disney executive that Michael Eisner swore would never become CEO. Yet Bob, who'd worked under the ABC and Disney brands for thirty years, had been slowly and effectively executing his responsibilities. Although Disney board members looked outside the company for a new CEO, they soon recognized that the right person might just be under their noses.

Bob Iger replaced Eisner and became the chief executive officer in 2005. During the previous three decades, he had had the opportunity to get hands-on experience in every facet of the television industry, from sports, to news, to entertainment. He was exposed to and participated in program acquisition, rights negotiations, and business affairs. And in most of this experience, he felt like a rookie being called up to the big leagues. Iger's autobiography, *The Ride of a Lifetime*, details how, at each stage of his career, he was asked to do something he'd never done before—and always on an increasingly larger platform with more stakeholders watching. For instance, when Capital Cities Communications bought ABC, it blindsided everyone in the company. Almost immediately, Bob was asked to become the president of ABC Entertainment. He writes in his book:

> It wasn't quite leaping without a parachute, but it felt a lot like a free fall at first. I told myself: You have a job. They're expecting you to turn this business around. Your inexperience can't be an excuse for failure.[1]

Bob Iger differentiated himself from the more experienced Michael Eisner in that he never left his humble, teachable mindset as he forged ahead. He remained authentic. He believed the first rule is to not "fake anything." He'd say:

> You have to be humble, and you can't pretend to be someone you're not or to know something you don't. You're also

> in a position of leadership, though, so you can't let humility prevent you from leading. It's a fine line, and something I preach today. You have to ask the questions you need to ask, admit without apology what you don't understand and do the work to learn what you need to learn as quickly as you can.[2]

THE PARADOX

Iger embodies a paradox I see uncommon leaders practice that sets them apart from old-school leadership, which is too often undermined by hubris and prevents such leaders from seeing certain realities.

Leading today requires combining these two attributes—confidence and humility. Reality changes so quickly, leaders cannot become arrogant, but must remain in a learning posture. At the same time, team members long for their leader to inspire them with confidence. Iger concluded, "There's nothing less confidence inspiring than a person faking a knowledge they don't possess. True authority and true leadership come from knowing who you are and not pretending to be anything else."[3]

When Capital Cities acquired ABC, Bob was called upon to lead the network, which represented the merger of both companies. Bob reminisces:

> Back then, the head of any of the (big) three networks was one of the most powerful people in television (a fact that seemed surreal to me), but to everyone in the industry, I was a looming question mark. I had no sense of how things were done in Hollywood, and no experience managing relationships with creative people or working with their representatives. I didn't speak their language. I didn't understand their culture. To them, I was a suit from New

> York who suddenly—for reasons that must have seemed baffling—had immense influence over their creative life. So, every day, I met with the managers and agents, writers, directors, and TV stars that Stu and Ted (my executive team) lined up for me. In most of those meetings, I had the distinct sensation of being poked and prodded in an effort to figure out who I was and what the hell I was doing there.[4]

I can only imagine what it must have felt like to be the executive leader but feel like the people under me were constantly questioning my right and ability to give them direction or to make good decisions on their behalf. It's a recipe for egos to flare up; to remind everyone who wore the badge and how the CEO had the right to fire anyone if he wanted to do so. This happens every year between executives and team members.

But Bob Iger refused to let his ego get the best of him.

Rather than trying too hard to impress whoever was across the table, he knew he needed to resist the urge to pretend he knew what he was doing. Instead, he asked a lot of questions, expressing his need for what others had to offer. This sort of expression is disarming to most humans. Bob knew when he arrived in Hollywood that he didn't have a big personality or any obvious swagger. He barely knew anyone in town. In light of this, he could either wilt under the power plays of agents and actors and display his insecurity, or he could leverage his "un-Hollywood-ness" to be a kind of mystery that worked to his advantage.

When Bob Iger became the chairman and CEO of the Walt Disney Company, he returned to the approach that had served him well. He didn't pretend to be Michael Eisner (which worked in his favor) or to be Walt Disney. He humbly demonstrated he was himself:

- He listened more than he spoke.

- He learned more than he taught.
- He sought to add value more than gain value.

And he won people over, one person at a time.

Because he led in this fashion, when he made a confident decision, people felt he was believable. His humility balanced his confidence and magnetically convinced others to side with him even when they saw things differently. His confidence was real but came in smaller doses, mixed with humble listening along the way. The fact is, each step along the way, people felt he wasn't qualified for the new job, and often Bob would smile and agree. Then he'd assume a learning posture with those very same people, all of whom agreed they wanted the company to flourish.

Bob built collaborators, not combatants. People didn't feel they needed to *compete* with him, but to *complete* him.

This was never clearer than when Bob Iger met with Steve Jobs to discuss how they could resuscitate the relationship between Disney and Pixar. When Michael Eisner led Disney, he and Jobs (original chairman of Pixar) represented two big egos at the table, both striving for the upper hand in the negotiations. I'm sure it felt like two male peacocks spreading their wings in pride to see who'd win the contest. Such displays usually result in win/lose equations.

When Iger took over, he contacted Steve to see if he'd meet with him. The two men didn't really know each other, so neither knew exactly what to expect, but in a relatively short time, Iger won Steve Jobs over. As you'd likely expect by this point, when he met with Jobs, Iger took a completely different approach:

1. Iger acknowledged he was in new territory.
2. He communicated that he wanted to add value to Pixar.
3. He said he felt unqualified to lead such an amazing brand like Disney.

4. He relayed his belief that both teams could be better if they worked together.

This effectively illustrates a helpful lesson for leaders. Leaders who are emotionally insecure will sabotage their ability to expand further or to go deeper in relationships. They will naturally put up walls, especially with competitive people. Potential partners are seen with suspicion, not expectation. Leaders perceive that strong counterparts represent one of three possibilities to them:

1. **Threat.** The person is a threat to their own power, position, and prestige.
2. **Thorn.** The person is simply viewed as a thorn in their side who must be removed.
3. **Thrive.** The person is seen as an asset who may enable them to improve and flourish.

Too often, Michael Eisner saw Steve Jobs as a threat. In contrast, Bob Iger saw how they could thrive together. Slowly, Iger began to undo the tangled knot created by the dysfunctional Jobs and Eisner relationship. Finally, one evening, Bob decided to float a crazy idea by Steve. Bob began by admitting it was a crazy idea. He suggested that maybe Disney could purchase Pixar. After a moment of silence, Jobs responded, "That's not such a crazy idea." Then, Steve explained that while he was open to dialogue, he would not make a unilateral decision without involving John Lasseter and Ed Catmull, Jobs's leaders of the Pixar animation team. Although it wasn't a crazy idea—it was a big idea. Bob agreed to meet with both men . . . and won them over. The purchase was made, and Steve Jobs and his Pixar crew joined the Disney empire.

How are you naturally perceived by others—as more humble or more confident?

What I love most about the deal was the way Bob won them all over. He told them if they'd sell Pixar to Disney, they would become the advisors for *all* Disney animation. After all, since Pixar led the way in computer animation, they should direct it all. In other words, the buyers became the learners. It was a picture of confidence and humility.

Over time, Bob Iger and Steve Jobs became friends. When Steve passed away in October 2011, Bob and his wife, Willow, were part of a handful of people who were invited to his memorial. They'd forged a partnership that Michael Eisner was unable to envision and had advised against. Why? The combination of humility and confidence seldom makes sense to those who don't possess it. It's hard to explain.

But allow me to try.

HOW CONFIDENCE AND HUMILITY CREATE MOMENTUM

Herein lies the big idea: uncommon leaders possess inspiring confidence yet express it with palpable humility.

In today's complex world, people look for anyone with a clear sense of confidence. Teams seldom move forward without seeing it in their leader. At the same time, people demand that a leader's confidence doesn't blind them to their own humanity. Leaders believe in themselves, but they don't believe they can do it alone. Dacher Keltner said, "The seductions of power induce us to lose the very skills that enabled us to gain power in the first place."[5]

Confidence plus humility furnishes the *energy of certainty* and the *flexibility of teachability* to create synergy in partnerships. Bob Iger found this to be true in his interactions with George Lucas (when he purchased Lucasfilm), with Ike Perlmutter (when he bought Marvel), and with Steve Jobs (when he bought Pixar). Bob was a learner but brought to the table enough confidence—even audacity—to make the pitch to these CEOs. Only confidence, even self-confidence, can catapult a leader from average to extraordinary.

THE ESSENTIAL ROLE OF CONFIDENCE

Because twenty-first century culture is increasingly uncertain and because our global economy is increasingly complicated and unpredictable, team members long for a sense of confidence. I believe one of the leader's tasks is to instill this in their team. This doesn't mean leaders have all the answers up front, nor does it mean they're absolutely certain everything will pan out according to plan. It simply means that, as our world experiences uncertainty, the human longing for confidence grows proportionately. Uncommon leaders understand this need and leverage it to increase their influence.

When leaders are confident, their symptoms of confidence become contagious:

- Their passion and energy become viral.
- Their clarity tends to motivate people to act.
- They pass on a sense of security to their team.
- Their sense of ownership expands to others.
- Their assurance that something must be done spreads.

Confidence can leak over time. The older we get, the more experience we gain, and the more cynical we become. After decades, our worldview changes; we no longer blindly trust others; we become self-protective; we see how selfish and immature even adults can be—and our confidence can wane. This is why a child can be so confident about skateboarding down a hill and his parents feel they must explain why he should be more careful.

Or a young girl can be so confident about her freedom on social media, blind to predators who prey on kids.

Confidence *reigns* in the young. And it tends to *wane* over time.

Consider how many movements in history were led by young, idealistic, energetic, and even naïve people. Along with that idealism comes confidence. And frequently, that confidence paid off. Joan of Arc. William Wilberforce. Martin Luther King Jr. Abolitionist movements. Women's rights movements. Voting rights movements. Civil rights and equal rights movements. Thousands of followers in those movements simply needed permission to act. And it was a confident leader (or leaders) who gave them that permission through their confidence.

The fact is, people follow confident leaders. Most people lack confidence and admire someone who's convinced and convicted to move in a certain direction. I believe people follow the leader who is clearest and most confident, not necessarily the one who is right. This is why religious cult leaders can gain a following—they attract unsuspecting people who crave confidence.

Let me focus in on why your people *want you* to be a confident leader. As our lives become more complicated and overwhelming, people feel they don't have time to research every decision they must make. We're tired and begin to look for "gatekeepers" who share our values and help us make good decisions. Celebrity endorsements. Wise authors. Social media influencers. Mavens. Political figures. Uncle Charlie. These "gatekeepers" become a sort of leader to us; such people do our homework for us and remove our need to think deeply about everything. We trust their opinion. When they're confident and can articulate their perspective, we feel comfortable moving in the same direction they're moving. They're often the ones who provide clarity in a confusing world, full of gray areas. The clear direction they offer makes us grasp what next step to take—and we like ourselves when we're clearer. This is why we value confidence in leaders.

For twenty years of my career, I served on John C. Maxwell's leadership team. John is an incredible author and a leader who seldom lacks confidence. He is a good thinker, he is a memorable communicator, and he is sure of his direction. When he makes decisions, he is clear and certain, even when he isn't always accurate. This not only has attracted a large staff, but millions of readers and followers over the decades. People value his confidence. Here are three observations I made as I served under him:

1. **His confidence was attractive.** As I mentioned above, those of us who possessed less confidence could borrow his and feel better about our lives. I recall attending a board of directors meeting when a "gray," even controversial, topic surfaced. A decision had to be made. Although several on that board saw the issue differently, John Maxwell listened then shared confidently why we should move in a certain direction. By decision time, everyone was attracted to his confidence and voted accordingly.
2. **His confidence was energizing.** Our team drew upon his energy, deriving from his confidence that our goal could be reached. We absorbed his energy and applied it toward our mutual objective. This was quite common. John Maxwell was once in a fast-food restaurant drive-through lane. When he got to the window, he asked if he could buy a simple cup of ice. No soft drink; just ice. The teenage clerk replied, "Oh, sorry, I can't do that." When John smiled and said, "Yes, you can!" she smiled back and said, "OK!" And John left with his cup of ice.
3. **His confidence invited ideas.** Because Maxwell was confident, we all felt it was worthwhile to apply

> our own ideas to the goal. After all, if we were sure to reach it, why not own it and add to it? John's confidence was the result of his emotional security. More than once, he'd share an idea for raising funds for a need around the world, and before we knew it, our entire leadership team was adding to his idea, building off of his belief that we could, indeed, pull it off. Time and again, I watched confidence breed creativity.

The truth is, confidence makes leadership believable. If people don't have a sense that you are confident—even self-confident—they may not have the confidence to follow you. If you don't believe in yourself, your people will find it difficult to believe in you. If you're tentative about your direction, your people will certainly be. Confidence usually comes first, even before competence (although both are essential).

In any case, leaders need confidence, and it's important we understand what our personal level of confidence is. In his book *Confident Leader!—Become One, Stay One*, my friend Dan Reiland suggests confidence isn't a topic most people think or talk a lot about. Most of us feel confident until we make some big decision like choosing a school for our child, buying a home, or taking on a huge project at work. Then, suddenly, we're different people. We don't want to look foolish by failing or fumbling or falling down. In these big moments, most of us shrink from our normally self-assured manner. I asked Dan what percentage of leaders he interviewed were over-confident and how many were under-confident. He believes about three in ten consistently struggle with over-confidence. Most of us have normal levels of confidence until we hit a wall. Then, about seven in ten struggle with under-confidence. We end up striving to construct a narrative of confidence inside ourselves and our team.[6]

BEWARE OF OVERCONFIDENCE

Unfortunately, over time and when left unchecked, confidence can morph into something unhelpful for leaders. This is what we call ego. It fogs our objectivity. It diminishes our logic. As leaders succeed, they become convinced they'll continue to win; some even blindly believe they can do no wrong.

The more we succeed, the larger our ego can grow. Momentum can cause us to look better than we really are. Over time, confidence can be fed by our egos and our egos by our confidence. There's a fine line between confidence and cockiness. In today's world, many among the emerging generation of young professionals see confident leaders cross that line and become arrogant. These leaders don't want to be questioned; they don't want any roadblocks in their way. They can suspect that if someone interrogates them, that person must not believe in their mission. The line is blurred between the organization's progress and people's submission to the leader. This kind of arrogance is nauseating. And this is the one big reason why humility plays a necessary role.

THE ESSENTIAL ROLE OF HUMILITY

In Jim Collins's classic book *Good to Great,* he introduced us to "Level Five Leaders." These are the ones who reached the top; the leaders who took their company from being "good" to being "great." His research team was shocked by what they found in these people. He expected those companies to be led by charismatic leaders, with huge personalities and even bigger egos. Instead, he found the opposite. They were leaders with a surprising sense of humility. They had no illusion they'd accomplished a goal alone. Collins wrote that when something went wrong, they looked in the *mirror* and said: "How can I improve to lead this team better?" When something went right, they looked out the *window* and said: "Look at this team. Look at what they achieved."[7]

Both confidence and humility are attractive, and doubly so when combined.

Humility makes your confidence believable.

When team members *only* see confidence, they begin to suspect you're not being honest; some piece of the puzzle is missing. They know all leaders eventually make mistakes, and followers begin wondering: When can I trust you? Confidence alone feels disingenuous.

When you demonstrate humility, you communicate credibility. Humility signals self-awareness and authenticity. A person who's always confident and has little humility creates suspicions in team members. Not unlike the person who always uses hyperbole to make their point. People stop trusting this kind of leader. They know their leader is human and begin thinking, "You can't be so sure all the time." Eventually, they stop taking the leader seriously.

Jason is a manager who faced this challenge last year. He was placed in charge of a team and immediately turned into the equivalent of a motivational speaker while in front of them. He talked about his big vision, about how great everyone was, and about how they could not fail. I spoke to his team members shortly after Jason took over. While every one of them appreciated his positive attitude, his certainty did not bode well. They were too savvy about the difficulties they regularly faced and didn't "buy" Jason's superficial confidence. He came across as naïve.

Jason needed a reality check.

I consulted with him and suggested he add humility to his magnificent attitude. If his team saw him acknowledge that their objectives were tough and there may just be some long days ahead—adding a word of confidence would have been just what they needed. He would have been believable.

Humility signals transparency and invites reciprocation. When you are humble, you display your humanity and acknowledge your imperfections. When team members see this, they're likely to volley it right back. Our brains are hardwired to do this. Belonging works from the outside in. When in groups, our brain lights up differently depending on the social cues we exchange with others. When vulnerability cues are sent, the amygdala switches from *protection mode* to *partner mode* in team members. It moves from "fight or flight" norms to understanding and empathy. Humility signals that you are a human first (before you're a boss) and invites others to connect and help. People want to reciprocate with transparency and trust.[8]

Alison Wood Brooks, from Harvard Business School, conducted an experiment that illustrates this. She described two scenarios to people and asked them how they would respond:

1. You are at a train station; it is raining. A stranger approaches you to ask: "Can I borrow your cell phone?"
2. You are at a train station; it is raining. A stranger approaches you to say: "I'm sorry about the rain. Can I borrow your cell phone?"

Later, Brooks asked her respondents how they believed the overall population might respond to this scenario. The vast majority predicted the scenarios wouldn't matter; either way, most people wouldn't give up their cell phone to a stranger. They were wrong. Brooks and her team found that a full 422 percent more people said "yes" in the second scenario than said "yes" in the first. A simple but clear signal of empathy and shared humanity made all the difference in the world. Suddenly, the person asking the question had become real and transparent.[9]

Humility makes you magnetic.

When humility is present alongside confidence it makes the leader easier to follow. It is attractive to people. Sometimes we don't know why we are drawn to humble leaders, but we are. We feel they are reachable, teachable, and touchable, not some prima donna who resides in an ivory tower. As I mentioned earlier, when humility is present, trust deepens among team members. When leaders are humble, they pull people toward them instead of pushing them away. NYU social neuroscientist Jay Van Bavel says, "The moment you're part of a group, the amygdala tunes in to who's in that group and starts intensely tracking them. These people were strangers before; now they're important to you. It's such a powerful switch; a total reconfiguration of the entire motivational decision-making system. The whole dynamic changes."

I have a theory I call "The Calcutta Paradox."[10] (It's one of our *Habitudes—Images That Form Leadership Habits and Attitudes®*.) What enabled Mother Teresa of Calcutta to attract so many people? It was the fact that she was humble and didn't like attention—that magnetically drew others to her. It was the fact that she *didn't* pursue fame that made her famous.

I believe people possess a sense of fairness inside them. Whenever a leader exaggerates their importance, others tend to want to downsize the inflated description to be more accurate. Similarly, when a leader brushes off their own importance with humility, downplaying their value, others listening see a void and want to fill it.

Andy is a friend of mine who's an author. Whenever I've heard him talk about one of his books, he tends to be humble and underestimate its value. Can you guess what others say when he does this? They want to rave about it, to right-size people's understanding. Why? Because the leader didn't do it. People tend to fill what is lacking in a leader's self-description and empty what is too full.

When we brush fame aside, when we downplay our accomplishments, it is winsome and magnetic to people.

Humility welcomes team members to help you lead.

When you're humble you invite the input and insight of those on your team. Working together is not a *contest* in which to compete; it is a *puzzle* you must complete. Eventually, you have other leaders helping you reach a shared goal, not merely hirelings working on your goal.

Years ago, engineer and designer Peter Skillman and his team decided to study teamwork. They experimented with students at Stanford, UC Berkeley, and the University of Tokyo, challenging them to build the tallest structure possible using uncooked spaghetti, masking tape, a yard of string, and a marshmallow. Skillman's study had less to do with the *task* and more to do with the *participants.* His team also gathered some kindergarten students to attempt the same goal with the same materials. They were testing how team culture emerged among the participants.

Can you guess who built the tallest structure?

In dozens of experiments, the kindergartners built structures that averaged twenty-six inches tall, while the business school students' structures averaged ten inches tall. Later, Skillman had attorneys and CEOs take on the kindergartners—and they lost as well. How did children defeat adults?

1. Adults engaged in what psychologists call "status management." They became preoccupied with recognition and aware of how they appeared to others.
2. Kindergarten kids engaged in shoulder-to-shoulder exploration. The children didn't care who had the idea or got credit. They focused on solving the problem.[11]

I believe Skillman's experiments are a picture of what natural humility accomplishes. When leaders drop pretense, they create the opportunity for their team to accomplish more than would otherwise be possible.

BOTH OLD AND YOUNG DESIRE HUMILITY IN THEIR LEADERS

Today, educated team members *desire* and often *demand* humility. I know six friends who've recently left their companies due to ego-driven bosses. Not long ago I met with team members who served as part-time and full-time employees in various industries. I asked them about their supervisors, and their responses were telling:

- "I think my boss just likes hearing himself talk."
- "My supervisor's ego is ginormous. I've learned to just smile and agree with him. But we all laugh at him behind his back."
- "I'm already looking for work somewhere else. She doesn't get me and doesn't care."
- "Everyone seems so fake where I work. I'd rather take less pay and work someplace where they keep it real and show a little authenticity."

These are comments made by staff from among the Millennial Generation and Generation Z. But these young team members aren't the only ones who recognize the problem of leaders who lack humility. I also took advantage of an opportunity to meet with senior citizens (all eighty years old or older) and asked them to reflect on their careers and bosses. Most of these people described their work experience with something like the following:

> Overconfident and ego-driven bosses existed back in my day, too. We didn't like them either—but decades ago, we felt we just had to endure them. We didn't want to lose our jobs.

Today, things are a bit different.

The demise of the overconfident leader has been evident all through history. Consider two Roman emperors, Julius Caesar (101–40 BC) and Augustus (63 BC–AD 14). Julius Caesar and Rome are synonymous. As a military leader, he conquered more territory than Alexander the Great. And he was genuinely better at stepping back from his conquest and organizing what he won. In the end, however, Julius Caesar came to believe that his success was the result of his divine status. His ego blinded him to the conspiracies going on behind his back. Those plots not only ended his career, but his life.

But it didn't have to be this way.

Caesar Augustus was different. He took reign after Julius Caesar and was arguably Rome's most successful manager of ambition and confidence. He led the biggest and most profitable empire in history for more than forty years, and yet, in spite of his success, he modestly referred to himself as Rome's *primus inter pares,* or "first among equals." Augustus kept a sensible perspective on himself. "Even though he became the undisputed ruler of millions and the richest man in the ancient world, he listened to others and understood the value of moving cautiously and thoughtfully on everything from building roads to conducting wars. His favorite expression was 'festina lente,' or 'make haste slowly.'"[12]

Augustus stands out because this kind of measured ambition plus genuine humility is rare, indeed, when it comes to leaders.

Today, overconfidence and ego show up just as consistently as in the past. Illustrations include Dennis Kozlowski who served as CEO of Tyco; Hank Greenberg, CEO of AIG; George Zimmer,

CEO of Men's Warehouse; and Sandy Weill, CEO of Citicorp. Look up their stories. They were ambitious conquerors who were brought down by their egos and hubris. In the end, these leaders focused on what flattered instead of what mattered.

Summary of this paradox

MY CONFIDENCE	MY HUMILITY
1. Makes my leadership believable.	1. Makes my confidence believable.
2. Communicates energy and certainty.	2. Communicates trustworthiness.
3. Fosters creativity and participation.	3. Fosters authenticity and participation.
4. Causes team members to be passionate.	4. Causes team members to be loyal.
5. Is contagious in others.	5. Is contagious in others.

HOW TO BE A CONFIDENT YET HUMBLE LEADER

As I close each of the chapters on these eight paradoxes, I will offer some ideas on how you can begin practicing these paradoxes in your own leadership.

1. When in decision-making meetings, argue as if you believe you're right, but listen as if you believe you're wrong.[13]
2. When in conflict with team members, be willing to lose a few battles to win the war. Predetermine what "hills you're willing to die on."
3. Remain teachable in new contexts, even from those under your care. Don't let your confidence prevent you from improving your own ideas.

4. Refuse to cross the line between confidence and cockiness. Confidence believes you can do the job. Cockiness believes it will be easy.
5. Don't confuse confidence with certainty. You'll frequently have to take action without certainty as a leader. Even when uncertain, remain clear and transparent.
6. Don't let humility become sheepishness. When we're sheepish, we are self-conscious, preoccupied with our own weaknesses. This keeps us from progress.
7. As you meet with teammates, you must know what you don't know and trust in what you do. Be clear on the difference between the two.
8. If you possess a strong ego on the job, take time to list your shortcomings and mistakes. Remind yourself of your humanity by reviewing these regularly.
9. When tempted to boast about what you achieved, instantly turn your focus to a team member and brag about them. Let someone else do your boasting.

Almost thirty years ago, I spoke at a chapel service before a ball game between the San Diego Padres and the Chicago Cubs. Ryne Sandberg was an all-star second baseman for the Cubs at the time. And he got paid very well for his skills. Unfortunately, that year Ryne was in a hitting slump and wasn't playing near his potential. He and I talked after the meeting and he confessed to me it really hurt to be doing so poorly but paid so well. He also told me it angered the fans in Chicago. Fans and reporters criticized him for being this highly paid athlete who didn't perform. And the ball club wasn't happy either. It was a difficult time for everyone.

Several weeks later, however, I remember reading how Ryne decided to handle his situation. In addition to improving his swing, he met with the general manager of the Cubs and offered a large chunk of his salary back to the team. Yes—you read that right. He told them he didn't feel right about taking millions of dollars when he wasn't performing up to his potential. He wanted to give some money back. Wow.

Needless to say, Ryne won the fans over by this act. Those who had booed him—were now praising him . . . even before he got his good swing back. Why? He assumed a humble position (even as he remained confident that he would regain his previous hitting prowess) and won their hearts.

Humility doesn't mean weakness. Next-generation leaders are strong and confident—but they're secure enough to see beyond themselves. They're not worried about their image. They know their value, but it isn't about them. They have nothing to prove, nothing to lose, and nothing to hide. The mission is bigger than they are.

THINK IT THROUGH, TALK IT OVER

- Do you know leaders who balance these two qualities well?
- Who do you know who struggles with either of the two?
- What do you struggle with in your leadership: humility or confidence?
- Why do you think keeping a balance between the two is so challenging?

PARADOX 2

Uncommon Leaders Leverage Both Their Vision and Their Blind Spots

Sara Treleaven Blakely graduated from Florida State University in 1993 and soon found herself trudging door to door as a salesperson, selling fax machines for Danka, an office supply company.

Just what every college graduate wants to do upon graduation, right?

Well, it turns out that Sara was good at it. By the age of twenty-five, she was promoted to national sales trainer at Danka and began teaching others how to sell their products. She remembers wearing professional clothes with pantyhose and nice shoes as she went from store to store, in the blazing hot Florida sun. The hose didn't look or feel good to her. While she could appreciate the advantages of pantyhose, she wondered if women might be willing to buy a version without their antiquated appearance. As she dreamed up the idea, she also thought of a name: an entirely new industry called "shapewear."

THE ORIGIN OF SPANX

It was at this point that Sara attended a private party and decided to try an experiment. She cut off the feet of a pair of pantyhose and wore them under a pair of slacks. The result? It achieved the look she wanted, but the stockings crept up her legs, making her feel uncomfortable. She continued to experiment and eventually created what she later called Spanx. (The original pair is now enshrined at her headquarters.)[1]

Her next step was to relocate to Atlanta and pursue this invention.

When she arrived in Atlanta, Sara was twenty-seven, with $5,000 in her bank account and a big vision. She immediately began researching how to best scale a piece of women's apparel that would be a combination of hosiery and girdle and be both comfortable and affordable. She drove to North Carolina, a haven for hosiery mills, to show them her prototype. One by one, she was turned down by every representative she met. During the visits, she recognized that every company was run by men—who obviously never wore the products they sold. Sara knew this would make her journey an uphill climb.

Sometime later, however, she got the break she needed.

One of the representatives had told his daughters about Spanx and they convinced their dad it was a great idea. He called her and Sara got the support she needed. (No pun intended.) Over the course of the next year, the prototype was modified and modified again. When Blakely felt she had a product she'd be proud to sell, she used her credit card and spent all of her savings to cover attorney fees and purchase a patent.

Have you noticed that when folks capture a vision, it often captures them right back?

HOW DO WE GET THE WORD OUT?

By now, Sara Blakely was consumed with the question: How do we sell these Spanx? They were different enough to catch the attention of a customer, but she couldn't scale well from her home. She needed distribution outlets.

True to form, Ms. Blakely took some unlikely next steps.

She arranged to meet with an apparel executive with the Neiman Marcus Group. Their luxury department stores are nationwide and perceived as a high-end shopping location for customers. Sara was given only a few minutes to explain Spanx, so she was understandably nervous. She labored to describe how her product was not a girdle, and not pantyhose, but was a new generation of both. Unfortunately, she didn't feel she was getting through to this veteran executive at their Dallas, Texas, offices. Finally, Sara gathered whatever gumption she still possessed and requested the representative join her in the women's restroom, where Sara promptly tried on her pair of Spanx right before the woman's eyes.[2]

Immediately, the benefits of Spanx were obvious.

Neiman Marcus chose to beta test selling Spanx in seven of their department stores. Sara instantly called friends in those areas and paid them to buy her product. When those stores couldn't keep them on the shelves, they ordered more. Soon, Spanx was picked up by Bloomingdale's, Saks, and Bergdorf Goodman. Momentum was beginning to build.

> Can you spot how both vision and blind spots benefited Sara Blakely?

Sara was now ready to advertise. She sent a basket full of Spanx to Oprah Winfrey, along with a note explaining what they did for women's self-confidence. In November of 2000, Oprah named Spanx one of her "favorite things" on her program. Next, Sara secured a contract with QVC to sell Spanx on television and sold eight thousand pairs in the first six minutes. Needless to say, she reached a tipping point, and the shapewear began to sell itself.

Sara Blakely is now a billionaire. In 2014, she was named one of the one hundred most powerful women in the world, by *Forbes*.[3]

THE POWER OF LEVERAGING BOTH VISION AND BLIND SPOTS

Sara Blakely vividly illustrates the potency of utilizing both a personal vision as well as personal blind spots. While they seem like an oxymoron, they are generally both at work when great leaders grow or start something.

Vision gives leaders (and teams) a direction, but blind spots are often the very motivator that enables them to approach an idea in an unconventional way—and believe they can pull it off. Most new ventures require a leader to possess a clear target they want to hit. At the same time, their inability to see all the obstacles or challenges ahead of time helps them to maintain their energy as they try to hit their target. In short, leaders usually have to *see something* and *fail to see something* to reach their goal.

- **Vision provides the target to hit.** Because leaders can see their objective, they possess lots of energy, furnished by their goal. They can envision the destination internally and it propels them.

  We cannot lead well without a clear and compelling vision. In the absence of vision, we can only manage people and situations, maintaining protocol. Team members need their leader to not only possess a vision, but to communicate it clearly so they can implement it. Sara Blakely could see the benefits of shapewear before anyone had yet confirmed the genius of her idea. She had the capacity to see something internally before it could be seen externally.

- **Blind spots provide the ability to try unconventional means to hit it.** Because leaders can't see how others have failed using orthodox methods, they may try new and unconventional routes to arrive at their desired destination.

  Blind spots are at the root of almost every new endeavor. The pain a leader experiences with current realities drives them to push forward without bothering to see all the ways it may not work or to notice how others tried and failed before them. Sara Blakely had no experience in the shapewear or pantyhose industry. She had, however, experienced the blazing Florida sun and knew there had to be a better way to look in hot weather. The pain of her present reality paired with the hope of a better future reality pushed her to progress toward her dream.

Once Spanx took off, Blakely fielded questions from salespeople, who marveled that she'd gotten the attention of an executive following a trade show. In other words, in the crowded space of those gigantic trade shows where thousands of vendors exhibit their wares, how was Sara Blakely able to differentiate herself and get a department store chain to listen to her and buy from her? Sara looked puzzled, explaining she'd never taken her product to a trade show; she didn't even know that was protocol. She simply went straight to the top.

Call it a blind spot.

Most veterans in the hosiery industry would not suggest the plan Sara implemented:

1. Bypass all trade shows and set up a meeting with a department store executive.
2. Send a basket full of your product to Oprah Winfrey hoping she'll like it.
3. Schedule a television time slot on QVC and sell as many products as you can.

Sara herself recognized the benefits of her blind spots. "Don't be intimidated by what you don't know." She once said, "That can be your greatest strength and ensure that you do things differently from everyone else."

Bingo. She illustrates the value of blind spots.

HOW LEADERS CAN BENEFIT FROM BLIND SPOTS

Blind spots prevent us from letting obstacles stop us.

Almost every entrepreneurial endeavor includes a story of how a founder or an original team had no idea what they were up against or had no clue what was ahead of them as they launched. Some of the surprises became stepping-stones their team used to make progress. But in most cases, early leaders share (in hindsight) that it was a much harder road than they first anticipated. Many might even say that, without the blind spot, they might have been too scared to begin.

Had they known what was coming, their ideas might never have gotten off the ground.

The competition to invent the airplane is a vivid example. Orville and Wilbur Wright had four significant competitors, the chief being the secretary of the Smithsonian, Samuel Pierpont Langley. This federal employee had government funding, which made him the odds-on favorite to achieve this goal first. Langley was already a prominent astronomer, but longed to become famous for something bigger, on par with Alexander Graham Bell or Thomas Edison. In the end, his federal grants sped up his work, but his ego slowed him down. Since his fame guaranteed his failures were going to be seen by many, he began fearing failure. This caused him to overanalyze his work and delay some of his trials.[4]

The Wright Brothers, on the other hand, were bicycle machinists who had been studying birds in their free time. (Their invention, if you recall, looked a lot like a flying bicycle.) Of the three problems that had to be solved to fly—lift, balance, and power—Orville and Wilbur focused on balance, while Langley focused on power. He had everything to gain or lose, while the brothers tinkered with their machine without the distraction of failure in their minds. Failures were simply new steps toward the goal. Flying, for them, was a metaphor: *You take off against the wind, not with it.* The Wright brothers believed in the words of Henry Ford, that "failure is simply the opportunity to begin again, this time more intelligently."

The blind spot helped them. They were the first in flight.

Blind spots spare us from the curse of knowledge.

Other benefits of blind spots are less obvious but just as important. Often, blind spots can speed up the project. Because the leader doesn't know everything about the endeavor, he or she can bypass hang-ups that slow others down. In my opinion, more original ideas face roadblocks due to the "paralysis of analysis" than anything else. It's not that people didn't think enough about the project, it's that they overthought it. Marketing consultants call it "the curse of knowledge." We get caught up on all we know, and fearing a failure to capitalize on our knowledge, we can miss an opportunity right in front of us.

Consider the pursuit of a digital encyclopedia.

Back in 1993, Microsoft launched its idea of a web-based encyclopedia called Encarta. Bill Gates and the Microsoft team tried to assemble the world's greatest experts on any subject and create a digital encyclopedia, using CD-ROMs at first. Obviously, this required a long and tedious process of collating both the experts and the information and placing them on one "gatekeeping" source. Because they were so smart, however, I believe they missed the fact that culture was evolving toward a model that crowdsources ideas, updates information, and doesn't require a gatekeeper.

How can you prevent your vision from blinding you from seeing other options?

Jimmy Wales and Larry Spanger bought into a different idea for a digital encyclopedia. Their technological underpinnings also have their roots in the year 1993 but were built off an early proposal by Rick Gates and the first "free range" proposal by Richard Stallman in 2000. Stallman felt that no central organization should control content or editing. He believed the platform didn't need to offer expertise; the emerging internet culture was its own "wiki" world where a website could allow collaborative editing of its content and structure by its users. When it launched, we came to know it as "Wikipedia."[5]

If you were to ask people to predict which of these two platforms would take off, most would have said Encarta. After all, it was built by brilliant experts and funded by Microsoft's huge budget. Few would have bet on a startup that built a system that relied on random "experts" to weigh in and update information from all over the world. But that's exactly what happened. Encarta ceased to exist as of 2009. Wikipedia's global monthly readership is over 500 million people, as of this writing.

Avoiding the curse of knowledge worked to their advantage.

WHY DO WE NEED BOTH VISION AND BLIND SPOTS?

As I mentioned earlier, the idea of "vision" and "blind spots" when used in tandem appears to be an oxymoron. How can someone have them both? The fact is, we all do. And to accomplish something significant as a leader, we likely need both.

Let me illustrate with an analogy.

When driving a car, we look forward to seeing the freeway ahead, but we also have blind spots, regardless of how many mirrors our vehicle has. It's hard to imagine driving a car without being able to see the road ahead of us—and in many ways, without being able to envision our destination. Driving is an experience of both short-term and big-picture vision. We envision the place we are heading to and what will happen when we reach it. People who are legally blind are not allowed to drive because they can't see enough of the road. (There's a difference between blindness and blind spots.) A GPS in our car makes the drive easier to see because it provides us with a picture of the turns we'll need to make and how long our road will be until we take our next turn. We even get an ETA on our journey.

At the same time, driving a car always involves blind spots. We generally learn about them when we first learn to drive a car. They're the interesting angles or locations we cannot see while making progress. Certainly, we must be careful that our blind spots don't kill us—but we all know they're part of the experience. The same is true for the human eye. Each one of your eyes has a blind spot created by the optic nerve. The point at which each connects to the retina creates an area that can't transmit the image that light projects on the retina, and hence, a blind spot. When we close one eye and look at what's in front of us through the other eye, there are certain objects in positions we can't see. Because most of us enjoy the use of both eyes, we don't notice our blind spots.

So it is with leadership. Vision and blind spots combine to create "rookie smarts."

CAPITALIZING ON ROOKIE SMARTS

As I interview uncommon leaders, both experienced and inexperienced, I notice they leverage their blind spots, along with their vision to consistently create the advantage of "rookie smarts."

Many say the key to their success was "rookie smarts." Let me explain.

"Rookie smarts" is a term tossed around in business circles today describing the effective ideas that new or young people come up with and attempt that seasoned veterans would never try. Why not? Because of their experience.

You may not be shocked to learn that the majority of today's emerging youth population see themselves as entrepreneurs. Seventy-two percent of high school students claim they plan to be an entrepreneur.[6] Instead of seeking that corner office in a large company, they envision creating or curating something and then selling it as a product or service. What's amazing is—sometimes their lack of experience is what makes them successful.

I believe "rookies" can leverage both vision and blind spots while leading. The good news is you don't *have* to be young to be this kind of rookie. Simply defined:

1. Vision enables rookies to see what others may not yet see.
2. Blind Spots prevent rookies from seeing what the experienced do see.

HOW VISION CULTIVATES ROOKIE SMARTS

Twenty-seven-year-old entrepreneur Ankur Jain explains it this way: "If they'll make the leap, young entrepreneurs are especially well-positioned to succeed. In every other industry, age equals success: the more experience you have, the more senior you are. Entrepreneurship is the one place where some of the youngest people are at the top of the food chain. Why? Because young entrepreneurs' inexperience is their greatest asset. They can come into an industry and ask questions about things that, for everyone else, have become unquestioned assumptions."[7]

What's more, young entrepreneurs are still unburdened by the accumulation of "stuff," including old ways of thinking and doing work, mortgage payments and bills, and lifestyle choices that are so entrenched, it's nearly impossible to dig out of them. Many have accurately noted, "A lot of people think innovation is thinking outside of the box, when in reality innovation comes from thinking about a problem from a totally different box."

HOW BLIND SPOTS CULTIVATE ROOKIE SMARTS

Some have noted the irony of it all is—*rookie smarts likely come from rookie ignorance.*

Life tends to work like this. Sometimes we benefit from not knowing any better. Those who work in the field of melittology study the anatomy of all sorts of bumblebees. They smile when they cite the scientific journals proving it is physiologically impossible for a bumblebee to fly. Their wings are too small, and their bodies are too big to give them lift. Yet, everyone knows that bumblebees don't read those journals. They just fly.

Knowledge, experience, and information are a blessing and a curse. They offer all kinds of guidance, but they also burden people with all kinds of boundaries and confinements. Author Mark Twain lived in the midst of the industrial revolution, when new inventions were popping up all the time. One of his favorite descriptions of what seemed to be happening was simply, "They didn't know it was impossible, so they did it."

FIVE STEPS TO DEVELOP ROOKIE SMARTS

So, what are the actionable steps old or young rookies can take to ensure they are smart? What is it that enables people like you and me to leverage both vision and blind spots?

1. **Look at industries that are stuck and need a revolution.** Be willing to step outside of your familiar or comfortable zone, where you've fallen into a rut in the way you think. Instead, look outside at industries that have stagnated or fallen into disrepute with consumers because they're in a rut: transportation, healthcare, social services, insurance, banking, and so on. Consider Uber and Lyft, which revolutionized the "taxi service" industry because they pursued it in a totally different way. Identify places you can solve new problems and serve new people.
2. **Listen well to people who are or could be customers.** The entrepreneurs who've surprised industries with their rapid success have been young and willing to listen. They're teachable. They want to attempt new services or products because the old ways seem so antiquated. (Think Baby Boomers who've insisted on continuing current methods in a time of rapid innovation and growth.) When I launched Growing Leaders, I did a listening tour among schools and businesses that enabled me to shoot out of the starting gate with a product most of them wanted.
3. **Interact with people outside the industry for ideas.** People inside any industry for more than ten years are often stuck in a rut of old paradigms. Muscle memory has been built and the minds of everyone

settle in on a normal way of doing things. When we talk to those outside an industry, we often gain ideas others cannot see. Paradigms can create expectations and they can limit them. Some of the best ideas that have helped me pursue my mission at Growing Leaders came from outsiders who'd never done what I do, but who asked questions that made me think differently. In many ways, Sara Blakely was an outsider to the women's apparel industry, but that helped her in the end.

4. **Combine various industry ideas to create a new one.** I mentioned the Wright brothers and their first airplane earlier. They inspired one of our *Habitudes*® called "Bikes and Birds."[8] Their invention was built from two worlds they knew well: their study of the flight of birds and their trade, bike repairs. They simply combined those two different worlds to create a third world—flying bikes. Three men combined their expertise in acrobatics, circuses, and gymnastics to create an entirely new form of entertainment, Cirque du Soleil. Its combination of talent was designed to challenge conventional circuses. Johann Gutenberg combined his love of reading and his work in a winepress to create the first printing press. Instead of pressing wine, he pressed words. He created a whole new industry that not only expanded literacy but changed the way information spread.
5. **Lead the way, by risking a prototype before it's perfect.** Most of the time, we must shoot bullets before cannonballs, says Jim Collins. By this he means we must begin to aim at a target and start hitting it with inexpensive prototypes (bullets)

> before using larger (and more expensive) ammunition. Don't try to be perfect right away. If you wait for perfection, you'll be left in the dust. Perfection comes later as you tweak the recipe. The reason so many startups today have succeeded is because a person entered an industry without the confinements or paradigms that constrain those currently trying to perfect an industry. They try something a different way to see what might work.

Twentysomething Emily Weiss created her makeup company, Glossier, in 2014, by following the steps above. During the course of her internships and early career, she recognized how most cosmetic companies sell products based upon women feeling bad about themselves. The subtext in the sale of these products is: *You're not good enough. You're not beautiful enough. You need help.* It's why fine cosmetic products cost a fortune. You're willing to pay anything to look better and feel better. High prices must mean high value, right?

Emily decided to do something radically different in the industry. She listened. To everyone. She claims to be addicted to Instagram, where she can hear from her followers and customers (her tribe). Many of her products originate with them. She asks questions then releases products they say they want: sunscreen that isn't sticky, greasy, white, or tinted, and doesn't smell like sunblock. Or skin moisturizer that doesn't cause you to break out. Glossier has created twenty-four products that are priced below those of major brand names, and the company has taken off. And it was all built by a "rookie" who was teachable.[9]

Her secret?

She *looked* and saw an industry that needed help. She *listened,* via social media connections. She asked a question about what product her followers really wanted and needed, and they responded. She interacted with outsiders to gain as much fresh insight and perspective as possible before taking action. She combined ideas to make new ones. Finally, she *led* the way. Glossier usually has a new product ready within months of its ideation. Without any experience in the cosmetics industry (she was a studio art major in college), she learned from mentors about scaling, capital investments, P&L, and so forth. All because she leveraged both her vision and her blind spots. It's an almost predictable pattern.

A WORD OF CAUTION

I would be remiss if I didn't pause and acknowledge the dangers of blind spots. Many leaders have been derailed because they allowed their blind spots to ruin them, personally and professionally. Succinctly defined, a blind spot is:

> An unrecognized weakness or threat that has the potential to harm not only the leader but their organization.

Case in point. Ron Johnson had served as an executive with Apple and Target when he was asked to take over J. C. Penney in 2011. At the time, Penney's felt they could benefit from Johnson's innovative ideas. Unfortunately, Ron entered the department store industry with several blind spots and never bothered listening to those who knew it well. He forced new, unconventional ideas into a new space and never heeded any warning signs. It was full steam ahead without even looking around. Ron Johnson was fired by his board in 2013, after Penney's stock had dropped 51 percent. One journalist summarized the disaster bluntly: "Penney 's got run into a ditch when Johnson took over. But rather than getting it back on the road, he essentially set it on fire."

FOUR TRUTHS ABOUT BLIND SPOTS

1. Our blind spots are often found conspicuously close to our strengths.
2. Blind spots may be undetected only to surface later in our careers.
3. Our blind spots have little to do with our intelligence.
4. Blind spots can serve to make us fearless, bold risk-takers, which can be both good news and bad news for our leadership.

When blind spots work for us, they often open up a new world that others can only imagine. In 2004, W. Chan Kim and Renée Mauborgne wrote a book entitled *Blue Ocean Strategy*. The authors argue that marketplace leaders can swim in one of two oceans:

1. A Red Ocean—colored by the blood of tough competitors struggling for market share in their crowded industries.
2. A Blue Ocean—clear, blue, and wide open because these leaders have created an entirely new industry that antiquates former competitors.

These leaders enter a "blue ocean" by the way they pursue their goal. It is both their unique vision and blind spots that enable them to create an ocean. Instead of creating a product or service that's just a little bit better than the competition, they engineer an entirely new way to solve the problem that current products are trying to solve.

Most of us know the story of Reed Hastings, an entrepreneur who rented a video cassette from a Blockbuster Video store in

1997, only to lose it and accumulate a gigantic late fee when he returned it. This problem sparked Netflix, a subscription model that would eventually stream movies. Reed conceptualized and later took it to Blockbuster. Unfortunately for them, Blockbuster felt they were doing fine and need not upgrade their system. The result? Reed Hastings launched Netflix, which took off and now enjoys a large part of the home entertainment market share. Blockbuster went from the record books to the history books in less than three decades.

iTunes created an entirely new way for consumers to access music in a world of records and compact discs. Digital downloads soon took over hard products. The unprecedented value iTunes offered triggered customers globally to flock to them, with recording companies and artists also benefiting. Partnering with iTunes, artists could receive up to 70 percent of the purchase price of digitally downloaded songs, hitting pay dirt in this new way of distributing music. Now operating in a crowded space that includes Spotify, iTunes continues to offer more than 37 million songs as well as movies, TV shows, books, and podcasts. It has sold over 25 billion songs, with customers downloading about 15,000 songs a minute.

> How can you prevent a blind spot from ruining you?

Canon's strategic move, which created the personal desktop copier industry, is a classic example of blue ocean strategy. Traditional copy machine manufacturers targeted office purchasing managers, who wanted machines that were large, durable, fast, and required minimal maintenance. Defying the industry logic, the Japanese company Canon created a blue ocean of new market space by shifting the target customer of the copier industry from corporate purchasers to users. With their small, easy-to-use desktop copiers and printers, Canon created new market space by focusing on the key competitive factors that the mass of noncustomers—the assistants that used copiers—wanted.

BALANCING YOUR VISION AND BLIND SPOTS

Both are obviously important but imagine an entrepreneur who dreams of inventing a product. He or she likely got the idea because they faced a dilemma or discomfort and knew there had to be a better way to address it.

- When horse-drawn carriages filled city streets with horse manure, men like Carl Benz and Henry Ford created horseless carriages—or automobiles.
- When Charles Kettering broke his arm turning the crank to get his car started, he developed an electronic ignition system for the modern automobile.
- Jacob Schick cut himself multiple times shaving and came up with a new kind of razor that is commonly known today as the Schick electric razor.
- Samuel Morse, like many others, grew frustrated with how long the postal system took to deliver a letter, so he invented the telegraph and Morse code.

There are two issues leaders must recognize when engaging in this process. First, the key to leveraging vision and blind spots is an often-neglected insight: *We must not fall in love with an idea but fall in love with a problem.* Ideas will come and go in our lives. They need to come and go, as new solutions surface that are more relevant and helpful. If we fall in love with an idea, we may be blinded to the better idea that comes along later. When leaders become passionate about a problem, they stay with it until they solve it, perhaps even again and again.

The Lean Start Up Company summarized the issue like this: "It's human nature to love answers, unfortunately that very tendency can prevent us from coming up with truly delightful solutions.

When faced with a problem, we tend to stop ideating as soon as we think we've found an answer. This Einstellung effect keeps us from finding the right solutions since our first ideas are rarely our best ideas. But it gets worse when we move forward into development and inevitably experience customer pushback; we would rather explain those issues away (sometimes even blame the customers) than go back to the drawing board."[10]

A second issue leaders face evolves subtly over time. Their obsession shifts from solving problems to generating revenue. While problems frequently lead to people creating solutions, once the process has begun, leaders often shift their focus too much toward money. Obviously, cash is needed to complete the new idea. When money is the chief focus, however, it's easy for leaders to wane in their passion for solving the original problem. Their passion drifts to an obsession to finding funding. The switch is natural, but sometimes deadly.

The good news is, every one of us can benefit from our vision and blind spots. Each of us can experience "rookie smarts" if we allow ourselves to live with this paradox.

Summary of this paradox

THE ROLE OF VISION	THE ROLE OF BLIND SPOTS
1. Provides a target to hit.	1. Opens you up to unconventional ideas.
2. Energizes a team.	2. Enlarges the team's options.
3. Constrains you to stay focused.	3. Liberates you to be creative.
4. Prevents you from playing defense.	4. Prevents you from limited thinking.
5. Enables you see what others cannot.	5. Enables you to avoid discouragement.

EIGHT KEYS TO NAVIGATING YOUR VISION AND BLIND SPOTS

1. "Marry" the problem you're trying to solve but "date" your methods. In short, to stay open to the best vision, stick to the need you wish to meet.
2. Invite outside points of view into the conversation. The best ones will likely come from a combination of insiders (which you already know) and outsiders.
3. Record what you learn from poor decisions. Failure is only a bad thing when we fail to learn from our mistakes.
4. Listen and learn from wise, experienced leaders anywhere you can. A lifelong learning posture is our only hope to thrive in the future.
5. Consistently mediate between self-doubt and self-confidence. Question yourself each time you draw a conclusion, but don't wane once you commit to something.
6. Keep reminders of your central vision in view. Most of us are visual people, who are energized by what we see. Make sure you can see the goal you want to reach.
7. As you make progress in your development, ask yourself:

   What needs a face-lift?
   What needs an overhaul?
   What needs a funeral?
8. Lead from within a balanced community. In other words, keep people around you that enable you to remain emotionally and socially healthy.

WHAT BOTH VISION AND BLIND SPOTS CAN PULL OFF

When Apollo 11 landed on the moon more than fifty years ago, it was a NASA mission many had thought impossible. It began with a speech by President John F. Kennedy who cast a clear vision of a lunar landing by the end of the decade. Volumes have been written describing how that vision catalyzed the NASA team in Houston. New technology was introduced, and new people were added as they shifted into high gear.

What may surprise you is that the successful lunar landing can be attributed to both vision *and* blind spots.

Those associated with the project revealed that Apollo 11 was successful because young people were placed in key leadership roles whose blind spots enabled them to push ahead when veterans would have pulled the plug during the space flight. The average age of the control center operators was twenty-seven years old. Many were even younger. Most had started as interns five years earlier and their job was to give tours of NASA, which forced them to know the precise function of each department. These twenty-seven-year-olds, just five years out of college, said it enabled them to succeed. Many of them assumed this was how careers worked: you get a big job with an important objective and you do it. What's more, those engineering and math majors were more poised than expected because they'd been using new computers in college at MIT. Since much of the other NASA staff were over forty years old, they were less familiar with the new technology and even doubted it was ready for a moon landing. The leaders at NASA saw a clear solution: those with blind spots were placed at the control center, while the veterans were tasked with guiding their work. One of the young operators recently admitted in an interview, "We didn't know what we didn't know . . . and audacity worked in our favor."

Just thirteen minutes before the landing, they almost aborted the mission. "We didn't want to lose Neil Armstrong and his crew.

It was the toughest period of the mission: the landing." Yet it was a twenty-three-year-old, Jack Garman, who played the big role in those vital minutes and kept them from aborting. "When most assumed we should stop, he said we should finish. He was cool as a cucumber." The youth paradigm wasn't cluttered with old ideas. It was fresh and ready to solve new problems with new ideas and new methodology.

Nothing pulls out the best in people more than a big goal with high stakes. Apollo 11 challenged a bunch of twentysomethings with the highest stakes of any project we'd ever seen. I believe people engage at their highest capacity with high stakes, a clear vison, and a few blind spots along the way.

THINK IT THROUGH, TALK IT OVER

- Do you know leaders who balance these two qualities well?
- Who do you know who benefited from their blind spots?
- What do you struggle with in your leadership: vision or blind spots?
- Why do you think keeping a balance between the two is so challenging?

PARADOX 3

Uncommon Leaders Embrace Both Visibility and Invisibility

Michael King Jr. was born on January 15, 1929, to parents from rural Georgia who had moved to Atlanta to make something of themselves. He grew up as a pastor's kid, but quickly observed some discrepancies in his dad's Baptist church that made him uncomfortable. The worship services were too emotionally driven for him, and he couldn't figure out why white people and black people remained segregated on Sunday mornings. Or, for that matter, at most other times.

At fifteen years old, Mike was intelligent beyond his years. America had joined World War II and many older teens enlisted in the military. To maintain enrollment, colleges began accepting juniors in high school if they could pass the entrance exam. Mike passed the exam and enrolled at Morehouse College at fifteen. He graduated at nineteen.[1]

It was at Morehouse College that Michael chose to become a minister. He decided the church offered the best opportunity to satisfy his "inner urge to serve humanity." He had made peace with the Baptist Church, and believed he'd be a "rational" minister with sermons that were "a respectful force for ideas, even social protest."[2]

From that point on, Michael King Jr. became a force to be reckoned with.

Michael King Sr., traveled to Europe in 1934 and visited the sites where protester Martin Luther launched the Protestant Reformation. Upon his return, he changed his name to Martin Luther King and his son's name to Martin Luther King Jr. King embraced his new name and became part of an entirely new protest and reformation—for civil and human rights.

THE YOUNG PROTESTER

In 1957, Martin King Jr., Ralph Abernathy, Fred Shuttlesworth, Joseph Lowery, and other civil rights activists founded the Southern Christian Leadership Conference (SCLC). The group was created to harness the moral authority and organizing power of black churches to conduct protests in the service of civil rights reform.

As a young leader, King chose to approach civil rights reform uniquely:

- Unlike his contemporary, Malcolm X, King felt he would gain sympathy from most Americans if he led his cause through nonviolent protests. He and his people were simply asking for equal rights and they did so peacefully.

The protesters were seen as rational.

- Counter to logic, King chose to intentionally walk into harm's way, which would draw media attention and allow the nation to witness the mistreatment of minority races. Television and journalists would be the best friends of the civil rights movement.

The protesters were seen as victimized.

- Instead of using divisive language, King appealed to American values, saying that the Boston Tea Party was an act of civil disobedience and what Adolf Hitler did was legal. He leveraged the Constitution and Declaration of Independence in his speeches.

The protesters were seen as patriotic.

- Contrary to rational thought, King utilized methods such as being arrested and thrown into prison (where he could not march or protest visibly) because he knew it would likely incite passion among his colleagues to stay involved.

The protestors were seen as noble.

King believed that organized, nonviolent protest against a system of laws, known as Jim Crow, which propagated Southern segregation, would lead to extensive media coverage of the struggle for black equality and voting rights. Journalistic accounts and televised footage of the deprivation and indignities suffered by Southern blacks, and of segregationist violence and harassment of civil rights workers and marchers, produced a wave of sympathetic public opinion that convinced most Americans that the civil rights movement was the most important issue in American politics in the early 1960s.[3]

King leveraged his actions and words, which, in turn, moved him and his cause forward. Author Garry Wills writes, "He literally talked himself into useful kinds of trouble. Like many prophets in the Bible, King did not aspire to the kind of leadership he finally undertook. He would gladly have fled the task, like Jonah. But the task pursued him." He goes on, "The orator's first test is to create heroes in response to his call. The orator's last test is his ability to create heroism in himself to match what he is preaching. Leaders and followers prod each other toward their shared goal."[4]

The crescendo of his career took place on August 28, 1963, at the March on Washington. Martin Luther King Jr. gave a speech we now call the "I Have a Dream" speech, which stands as one of the most iconic addresses in American history. Following that speech, King began to leverage both his presence and lack of presence in the movement to catalyze it forward.

Dr. King reminds us of another paradox in uncommon leaders.

THE PARADOX OF BEING VISIBLE AND INVISIBLE

Martin King was always aware of his influence. Even as a kid growing up in school, he saw his impact, for good or for bad. And he wanted to use it for good. He wrote, "If I were a minute late to class, I was almost morally conscious of it and sure that everyone noticed it. Rather than be thought of as always laughing, I'm afraid I was grimly serious for a time. I had a tendency to over-dress, to keep my room spotless, my shoes perfectly shined and my clothes immaculately pressed."[5]

Twice as a youth, King tried to commit suicide, because he thought he'd caused the death or sickness of a family member. He threw himself out of a second story window assuming he had influenced a tragedy. Fortunately for all of us—those attempts failed. But they illustrate that young King was deeply aware of the impact of his life and his words.

Later, however, Martin recognized that he could influence by both his *actions* and his *absence.* At times, people needed to see him set an example, and later they needed him to let them do it themselves. He needed to model the way and get out of the way.

In the beginning of any mission, most people need a visible leader, demonstrating what to do and clarifying the goal. Over time, however, those people need the leader to step aside to let them realize their potential. Ownership must be transferred. Leaders must be necessary—yet eventually work themselves out of a job. Good ones are irreplaceable at first, and then eventually replaceable. They recognize when they need to be heard but are quick to shut up when it's time. They're most helpful when people barely know they exist and start to believe they did it themselves. *It's not about the leader but the team and the mission.*

These people lead—and then get out of the way. In short, they embrace the paradox of being both visible and invisible, at the right moments.

Martin Luther King did this magnificently.

HOW KING LEVERAGED VISIBILITY IN HIS LEADERSHIP

In the beginning, Dr. King knew he had to take initiative in the difficult, uphill climb toward equal rights for all Americans. Many citizens had no idea what injustices were taking place in the South and would never travel to Alabama, Mississippi, or South Carolina to witness them. King's leadership had to be visible for both his followers (*who were often minorities and needed a model to follow*) as well as for most Americans who were complacent regarding civil rights. (*Because they couldn't see it, it wasn't their problem.*) Without visible leadership:

1. Blacks could have remained fearful and stayed uninvolved.
2. Whites could have remained apathetic and stayed uninvolved.

Between 1955 and 1965, Martin Luther King utilized his *visibility* to motivate minority races to get involved in the civil rights movement and to cultivate sympathy in the majority of the American population. Up until then, demonstrations were sporadic, often chaotic, and lacked a clear leadership philosophy. Here are examples of how he changed this:

King organized peaceful marches for blacks' right to vote, desegregation, labor rights, and other basic civil rights. Most of these rights were successfully enacted into the law of the United States with the passage of the Civil Rights Act of 1964 and the 1965 Voting Rights Act. During the march to Montgomery, Alabama, violence by state police against the peaceful marchers resulted in much publicity, making Alabama's racism visible nationwide.[6]

King willingly was arrested and went to jail or prison twenty-nine times in the course of the civil rights movement, often for the sake of setting an example for those who watched. He knew words were not enough to spark change; it required an example of sacrifice and suffering. King even wrote *Letter from Birmingham Jail* during one of his seasons of incarceration.[7]

King leveraged photos and media coverage, such as the famous 1963 image of the police dog jumping on a Birmingham teenager, Walter Gadsden, to win the hearts of those who saw the pictures. While fire hoses spraying water on protesters were not pleasant, photos and film of such events would frame the civil rights argument for millions.[8]

King's intent was to provoke mass arrests and "create a situation so crisis-packed that it would inevitably open the door to negotiation." He and other SCLC members chose to hold "sit-ins," demonstrations, and marches against laws they deemed unjust. He would let the public decide if they were correct after witnessing them.[9] And it worked. The Birmingham campaign was a success: Police Chief "Bull" Connor lost his job, the "Jim Crow" signs came down, and public places became more open to blacks.[10]

King agreed to be the visible leader to meet with Presidents Kennedy and Johnson, and other federal officials between 1961 and 1968. In these instances he believed that only he could accomplish their goals and should not delegate. Photographs of King with the presidents demonstrated to everyone how negotiation played a role in public policy change.

How have you intentionally leveraged your personal example to influence others?

Finally, King was visible to an entire nation in August 1963, making the speech that argued for civil rights for everyone. King's demands for equality braced people for a *new normal* by reminding them of *old commitments,* identifying their own voice in America's founding documents. He reassured them they were being true to themselves . . . not giving in to others.

The civil rights movement would not have taken such giant leaps forward during that decade had it not been for the visible example of Dr. Martin Luther King Jr. He won a Nobel Peace Prize for his work in 1964.

THE NEED FOR VISIBLE LEADERSHIP FROM YOU

In the early stages of your leadership, people need you to be visible. Most human beings are "settlers" who need "pioneers" to go first. They need someone who "knows the way, goes the way and shows the way for others," to quote my mentor John C. Maxwell. This has little to do with IQ. Most followers can figure out how to apply words of instruction. It's simply that *human example* is so much more powerful than *human explanation* in transforming behavior.

People would rather see a sermon than hear one.

Just like children need more than good lectures from their parents, team members need examples of behavior in organizations. It has been said that young people have never been good at listening to their elders, but they have rarely failed to emulate them. This could be said of leaders and teams. People do what people see. Most people are visual learners and learn best from example.[11] Uncommon leaders empower initially by modeling the way:

- They embody the vision that their team is attempting to achieve.
- They pick up trash in the parking lot to model servant leadership.
- They tend to the details, so people see that every little action matters.
- They demonstrate what they'll soon delegate to others to ensure quality control.
- They make the tough call (*hard decisions*) to show they're willing to pay the price.

When leaders practice this, their mission and their values take on deeper meaning. They become more believable and carry greater moral authority. Why? Because they practice what they preach. When you're visible, your words become more believable. We've all heard the phrase "You have to walk the talk." I have noticed that the more you walk, the less you need to talk. Visible leadership deepens your credibility in the minds of your people. Mahatma Gandhi's life was a model for Martin Luther King Jr. King studied Gandhi's writings, examined photos, and met with his family in 1959. During the sit-ins, hunger strikes, and the Salt March of the Indian revolution, Gandhi exemplified integrity and tangibly demonstrated what he asked of fellow protesters. This was never clearer than one afternoon when a woman brought her young daughter to Gandhi and asked him, "Would you tell my little girl to stop eating so much candy. She's consuming far too much sugar."

Gandhi thought for a moment as he rubbed his chin, then replied, "Come back in two weeks."

The mother was confused, but realized Gandhi was not going to speak with her or her daughter on that day. After two weeks, the woman returned with her child and asked him again to speak with her. This time, Gandhi knelt down at eye level with the young girl and requested that she stop eating so much sugar. The girl agreed and ran to play with other children. Perplexed, the mother inquired, "Why didn't you just tell her two weeks ago?"

Gandhi smiled and replied, "Because two weeks ago, I ate too much sugar."

The Indian leader would not ask anyone to do something he wasn't first doing himself. He recognized the power of visual leadership, not just verbal leadership. This is paramount in our day, when our world claims to celebrate authenticity but, in reality, promotes facades. Consider social media. Millions of posts are:

- Filtered photos that are doctored and unreal.
- Full of hyperbole and irate reactions rather than rational communication.
- Artificial Instagram accounts, called "Finsta," that offer false personas.
- Fake news, where "journalists" leverage clickbait to get us to read a post.

Our world is crying out for leaders who practice what they preach.

Broadcast media is chock-full of examples of poor leaders in government, business, academia, and nonprofit work.

Incompetence is not hard to find. I believe, however, there may be something even worse than a typical incompetent boss: "absentee leaders." I brought this up in the first chapter. These leaders are not necessarily misbehaving, yelling, or making bad decisions. The *Harvard Business Review* reports, "Absentee leadership rarely comes up in today's leadership or business literature, but research shows that it is the most common form of incompetent leadership."

These leaders are absent in many ways—sometimes physically, emotionally, volitionally, or mentally.

The CEO of Hogan Assessment Systems, Scott Gregory, writes, "Absentee leaders are people in leadership roles who are psychologically absent from them. They were promoted into management and enjoy the privileges and rewards of a leadership role but avoid meaningful involvement with their teams. Absentee leadership resembles the concept of rent-seeking in economics—taking value out of an organization without putting value in."

This issue is both blatant as well as ubiquitous, which is why it belongs on our list of paradoxes. While no one enjoys being micromanaged by their supervisor, a 2015 survey of one thousand working adults showed that eight of the top nine complaints about leaders concerned behaviors that were absent; employees were most concerned about what their bosses didn't do. Clearly, from the employee's perspective, absentee leadership is a significant problem, and it is even more troublesome than other, more overt forms of bad leadership.[12] Research shows that being ignored by one's boss is more alienating than being treated poorly.[13]

WHY YOUR VISIBLE LEADERSHIP IS PARAMOUNT

1. *Leadership operates on the basis of trust.* People will follow you only as closely as they trust you. When

you model what you require your team to do, you earn the right to be followed. Trust is the currency, and your example is your bank account.

2. *Leadership naturally stems from moral authority.* Words can influence temporarily, but long-term influence is the result of seeing a leader's lifestyle. Genuine credibility emerges from the moral authority we earn through action.
3. *Leadership's gauge of effectiveness is the followers.* I call it *the Mirror Effect.* If you want to know how effectively you lead, your people are a mirror. They'll reflect you. Within twelve to eighteen months, teams mirror the attitude and values of their leaders.

N. Dean Meyer and Associates consulting firm made a remarkable discovery years ago. When companies want to change their organizational culture, they can do so in one of two ways:

1. The executives can meet, create a new set of core values, frame them, and hang them in various places on the wall. This method takes ten to twelve years to transform the culture.
2. The executives can meet, create a set of core values, but then attach three actionable items to each value that the executives practice regularly in front of the team.

This second method transforms the culture in less than three years. People do what they see.

THE NEED FOR INVISIBLE LEADERSHIP

Over time, as I mentioned earlier, uncommon leaders recognize they must trust that their example has taken hold and step out of the way for others to step up.

I learned this firsthand in my own nonprofit organization, Growing Leaders. I started it in 2003, with three friends who became my first board members. As we grew, I added staff members, and we began serving universities, businesses, K–12 schools, professional sports teams, and other nonprofit organizations who wanted a leader development system that was engaging and unique (image-based learning courses, called *Habitudes*®).

How have you embodied this truth? Where have you failed?

From the beginning, I did my best to create and embody our mission and core values. I wrote the content, worked with designers and publishers to create and distribute it, and developed the systems to deliver it to teams of learners. When it became popular across the country (and even in seventy-two countries), I was in a quandary between my insistence on quality control and my desire to scale our work. I had to replicate myself; I had to find others who'd serve with me to scale our mission. I had to find like-minded people who could do what I did, but this was hard for me.

It was not unlike thousands of organizations around the world.

Two years ago, our growth plateaued for the first time in years. Our expansion had been up and to the right for over a decade, but it had leveled off. I didn't like it. Each one of us knew it was time for a reorg. We needed to rearrange our team and tasks if we were going to grow again. It was "fruit basket upset."

- Our flow chart changed.

- We let some people go.
- We hired some new people.
- We repurposed job descriptions.
- We added departments.
- We changed our distribution models.
- We created new systems.
- And most of all, I felt I needed to lead in a different manner.

We were progressing from the "Go Go stage" to the "Adolescent stage" of our organization's life cycle. These are terms coined by author and consultant Ichak Adizes, the founder and CEO of the Adizes Institute, and one of the world's leading management experts. Dr. Adizes developed a chart for leaders to recognize their organizational life cycle and what stage is on the horizon. Organizations begin in the "Infant stage," then move into the "Go Go stage," before entering the "Adolescent stage" of their growth.

Infant organizations are at risk for not having enough cash. Go-Go organizations are at risk for too many opportunities. To shift into the Adolescent stage, the leader and team must focus. They must say "no" to many opportunities that fall slightly outside their expertise. Go Go organizations operate on the belief that more is better. Adolescent organizations operate on the belief that better is more. They go deep in order go wide. They go slow to go fast.

My job, as founder, is to relinquish *control* and even *creative license* to team members. This means I must move from solely *visible* leadership to *invisible* leadership. I must step away for them to step up. And just as they needed me to demonstrate visibly what needed to be scaled, now my job is to become invisible—so they can do just that.

Let's return to Dr. King to see how he accomplished this.

HOW KING LEVERAGED INVISIBILITY IN HIS LEADERSHIP

By the mid-1960s, Martin Luther King Jr. began to sense the civil rights movement had reached a tipping point. He also began to sense his life was vulnerable. He all but predicted his own death. He became consumed with ensuring other leaders—often younger ones—began to step up to positions of influence. If he didn't step aside a bit, they'd always depend on him to lead the way; to run point; to go first. Note the steps Dr. King took.

As I noted earlier, Dr. King was arrested and jailed a total of twenty-nine times. Part of his reason was to model sacrifice for other civil rights participants. At times, however, he leveraged his incarceration to step back and force others to fill roles, to have a voice, and to influence the movement. His presence was so large that others may not have realized their potential if he hadn't withdrawn.

> How have you intentionally stepped aside to challenge others to step up?

After he made speeches—where he was visible and audible—Dr. King would often move quickly away from the spotlight so that the movement didn't keep the spotlight on him and his charisma. In short, he used his presence, then his own absence, to mobilize others to step up into roles of influence, at the appropriate time.

Over the years, Dr. King made decisions on whether to be present or not at meetings, often based on whether those attending needed their own voice to be heard. Debates took place over the issues of the movement and Martin wanted to ensure his presence wouldn't distract or intimidate others or unnecessarily induce people to depend on him.

Practicing this paradox works a little like parenting. When your children are toddlers, they need lots of direction and intervention. As they mature, our leadership style changes in our home. Kids become more independent and require less intervention (at least they should). They need less direction and more delegation. Less telling and more asking. Less explaining and more experiences to develop them. And no parenting act provides a more vivid illustration of this than teaching a child to ride a bike.

Consider this leadership process.

Most young kids don't start with a bicycle but with a tricycle. The three-wheeled trike enables them to get used to peddling without much risk of falling down. Later, however, this gets boring. They want to upgrade to a bicycle, which has only two wheels. But because this requires balance, we launch them with a bike that has training wheels. They now get used to peddling and balancing themselves. Eventually, however, they want those training wheels to come off. At this point, our leadership is a tender balance of *support and letting go.* This is precisely what's required of us as we lead our teams. Support and letting go.

MOVING FROM EMPOWER BY EXAMPLE TO EMPOWER BY EXPERIENCE

So, let's talk about this paradoxical juggling act of visibility and invisibility. When do we know it's time to move from empowering people by our "example" to empowering them by their "experience"? To be clear, I don't believe it's cut and dry, black or white, or overnight. Instead, over time, teams will eventually require leaders to take a risk and let them do what only the leaders once did. Let's talk about some fundamental signals that the time is right.

When it's time to move from empower by example to empower by experience:

1. People have watched you do it numerous times.
2. People know the routine and can articulate it to others.

3. People have had the chance to try it themselves.
4. People display that they're convinced of the legitimacy of the mission.
5. People have built muscle memory from the task.

As I mentioned earlier, our nonprofit organization is a content company. As a result, the content we publish and broadcast is extremely important to me. I insist on quality presentations at events, excellent blog articles, e-books, curriculum, and trade books. They all reflect our brand at Growing Leaders.

Five years ago, Holly, our COO at the time, and I noticed that I was speaking at about one hundred events each year. And like the rest of humanity, I was not getting any younger. We had a handful of other speakers, but I needed someone to begin investing in so that he or she could share the load of content creation and delivery. I needed someone who could do what I do in his or her own style. It was at this point I invited Andrew McPeak to join our team. He was a contract worker who began working with me to write and speak. Over time, Andrew's ability to create content expanded. He now writes and speaks on most of the topics I speak on, and often does a better job than I do. Audiences really enjoy him.

Last year, we named him Vice President of Content.

While I am still writing books, speaking at certain events, creating articles and e-books, Andrew oversees this effort. He and I co-lead our Growing Leaders podcast, we co-authored books, and he keeps getting better and better. And I am learning to become more invisible.

WHAT ARE THE ESSENTIAL INGREDIENTS?

When I see leaders practicing this paradox in a holistic way, they always include four elements in the process. It is the formula for developing talent and preparing to become "invisible." The formula involves practicing these four elements we'll call:

The Big IDEA

I—Instruction. Leaders must provide verbal insights and explanations through discussion. This furnishes teams with insight on "why" as well as "what." This interaction can happen in a training room or anywhere with a goal to guide their learning process. We use images, metaphors, and memorable phrases that summarize concepts for them. *People need conversations.*

D—Demonstration. Leaders must find ways to model what the insight looks like in real life. This furnishes teams with confidence and vision. This example can be as simple as watching someone—in person or on video—practicing the visual concept people need to learn. It is an important element because "people do what people see." *People need observation.*

E—Experience. Leaders must turn teams loose to practice the insight on their own; to apply the knowledge. This builds skills and abilities. I believe learning isn't complete until people have executed tasks for themselves. This process ensures that theory becomes practice. If teams often lack experience today, it's because we fear they won't execute it perfectly. *People need application.*

A—Assessment. Leaders must take time to debrief and evaluate the learning outcomes with teams. This furnishes them with wisdom and perspective. I don't believe experience is the best teacher; I believe experience plus evaluation is the best teacher. We must take time to assess what happened so that people gain helpful insight from their practice. *People need evaluation.*

As you consider the balancing act of visibility and invisibility, keep in mind all four elements above are necessary. The first two are about what *you* do; the second two are about *them.*

I have been speaking on a regular basis since I was seventeen years old, thanks to Shawn Mitchell. Shawn launched an outreach to kids in San Diego that year (1977) and asked me, a high school student, to help him. (I was the same age as many of the teens we served.) Each week, on Friday nights, we showed a great movie that contained a life principle within the story, then Shawn would hop onstage to speak, sharing a corresponding message and application for the audience. As his protégé, I helped set up the room, get him some water, and tend to details. Each week, I'd watch Shawn passionately engage the audience, bringing them to a practical action step by the end. He was—and still is—a dynamic communicator.

How could you creatively practice these elements?

Several weeks into our Friday night outreach, Shawn met me backstage and spoke to me in a raspy voice. He was almost whispering when he said, "Tim, I don't think I'll be able to speak tonight. Something's wrong with my throat. Uh, you're going to have to speak tonight."

My eyes grew large, as I replied, "Shawn—I don't speak. I get you water!"

But, alas, I was the most logical alternative. So, I looked over his notes, and that very night, I spoke to a large audience for the first time in my life. I'm sure my knees were weak, my voice stammering, and my body shaking as I plodded through my "motivational" speech. But I made it. Afterward, Shawn gave me a bear hug and affirmed my skills, saying, "Tim, you were great.

From now on, we're gonna rotate. I'll be on one week and you'll be on the next."

Thanks to Shawn, I have been communicating to large audiences for more than forty years.

What I love most about my friend and former mentor Shawn is this. A few years ago we met for dinner to reminisce about that Friday night outreach. As we discussed our memories of my first night speaking, Shawn gazed downward, unable to give me eye contact. I asked what was wrong. When he looked up, he smiled and said, "Tim—I have a confession to make." He paused, then went on. "I didn't really have laryngitis that night. I was fine. But that was the only way I knew I could get you onstage. If you knew I was able to speak, you would not have gone through with it."

At that point, I didn't know whether to laugh or be grateful. I love the fact that Shawn's goal that evening was not to put the most effective communicator onstage. If that were his goal, he would've spoken. His goal was to develop a young leader who needed to prove himself. You might say his goal was to move from a visible to an invisible leader.

Summary of this paradox

WHEN I AM VISIBLE	WHEN I AM INVISIBLE
1. I inspire people by my example.	1. I empower people by my delegation.
2. People grow confident in my leadership.	2. People grow confident in their ability.
3. I am a model for others.	3. I am a mentor for others.
4. My team begins to believe in me.	4. My team begins to believe in themselves.
5. I give people an example.	5. I give people an experience.

The habits and attitudes of a visible yet invisible leader

1. Examine your core values. Then, assign three actionable steps you can take, as their leader, to model what those values look like in real life. Practice them regularly.
2. Note where you see team members are falling short. Then, identify actions you can take to demonstrate how staff can rise to the challenge and embody the culture.
3. Reflect and note the areas in which it is most vital to be visible in your leadership. What's most crucial to accelerate the mission? What ways can you exemplify that?
4. Don't confuse words and actions. Whenever you communicate a key message, find ways to make it a "show and tell" (words *and* actions) not just "tell and tell."
5. Identify team members who need to step up to a higher level in their leadership. Discuss this with them then choose to be absent from meetings so they can step up.
6. Find one way you can move from "visible to invisible" leadership in the areas you are most natural and prone to cling to. How can you relinquish what you like to possess?
7. Meet with an accountability partner to discuss what prevents you from moving to invisible leadership. Is it ego? Is it fear? Inflexibility? Are you a creature of habit?
8. Take the big "IDEA" we discussed earlier and list steps you can take to embody each word: instruction, demonstration, experience, and assessment. Then, follow through.

A visible to invisible speech

Dr. Martin Luther King Jr.'s seventeen-minute "I Have a Dream" speech in August 1963 illustrates this marvelous paradox. It was during the March on Washington, held one hundred years after Abraham Lincoln's Emancipation Proclamation—and the message was: *We're still not completely emancipated.*

King knew when to linger and he knew when to leave.

There were ten speakers in the lineup that day, most of them desiring a morning time slot, while the audience was still fresh in that August heat. King said, "Just put me where you see fit." He spoke last that day. His manuscript would require eleven minutes. He felt the speech should be lower-key, since he was speaking to a broad audience about controversial times. He decided to talk about America's "bad check" with insufficient funds. When he finished, however, he realized his listeners hadn't experienced an "aha" moment. He looked up from his script and read the crowd, then heard Mahalia Jackson cry out: "Tell them about your dream, Martin!" Jackson was a Grammy Award winning gospel singer who'd sung earlier that day. She was referring to a speech King had given in Detroit sometime earlier where he shared his dream of equality.

King's advisor, Clarence Jones, said, "Then he takes the written speech he prepared, and he slides it to the left side of the lectern, grabs the lectern, looks out on more than 250,000 people there assembled." Jones remembers turning to the person next to him and saying, "These people out there, they don't know it, but they're about to go to church."

King was constantly reading his followers' need for visibility or invisibility from him. He realized he wasn't finished. They still needed a visible leader.

Extemporaneously, Martin began passionately painting a picture of his dream for another six and a half minutes (his speech took seventeen and a half minutes), moving his audience with his metaphors and casting a vision of what the future could look like. When he felt satisfied that the divine "aha" had occurred, King said, "Free at last, free at last. Thank God Almighty, I am free at last."

And he walked quickly away from the podium, moving again from visible to invisible.

THINK IT THROUGH, TALK IT OVER

- Do you know leaders who balance these two qualities well? How do they do it?
- What do you struggle with in your leadership: visibility or invisibility?
- In what areas do you rely on words more than actions to motivate your team?
- How could you improve on preparing potential leaders and getting out of the way?

PARADOX 4

Uncommon Leaders Are Both Stubborn and Open-Minded

I met Truett Cathy in 1997 when I moved to Atlanta. I shook his hand at Chick-fil-A's headquarters after eating my very first Chick-fil-A sandwich there. (Having lived in San Diego and Denver before that, I'd seen no Chick-fil-A restaurants yet.) He smiled and welcomed me to town as if he were the mayor. I watched him model a unique kind of leadership over the next fifteen years and was honored to attend his ninetieth birthday party. It was big.

Before he passed away on September 8, 2014, Samuel Truett Cathy had written six books, won numerous awards, visited presidents in the White House, appeared on television, and had just retired from his privately owned restaurant company that made nearly $6 billion every year and was growing fast. Last year the chain reported a record 54 percent growth in profits. Amazingly, Chick-fil-A has more than doubled in total revenue since Truett retired.

You might have never guessed this was coming when he was growing up.

While we remember Truett Cathy as the founder of Chick-fil-A, he started small and slow in 1946. He ran a single restaurant for a decade, tweaking the recipe for his chicken, his vision, and his values and how he would expand his privately owned company when it became a franchise.

Most people do not realize the hardships he endured during his early years.

- His father left the family when Truett was in primary school.
- The entirety of his teenage years was spent during the Great Depression.
- He served in the US Army during World War II, from 1941–1945.
- He sold his car to start a small restaurant, the Dwarf Grill, with his brother.
- His brothers (Ben and Horace) died in a plane crash in Dalton, Georgia, soon after.
- He endured a fire early on that, in many ways, forced him to start over.

Truett later said if he'd known what he would go through at the beginning he might have never started. The truth is, however, that every obstacle, every failure was a lesson. Each one taught him either *how he needed to adapt or how he needed to cling to what he knew to be right.* Truett Cathy believed if you are not willing to fail, you're not ready to succeed. Looking back, he is glad he didn't know what was coming. He was only twenty-five. It kept him in the game. Life is to be lived one day at a time. Truett continued to try things he never saw anyone do before—like creating his original chicken sandwich and placing a chicken restaurant in a shopping mall.

Over the years, I noticed two incongruous traits in him. He possessed an absolute stubborn will regarding the ideals he considered essential, while simultaneously modeling adaptability and an open mind when it came to growth, keeping up with the times, and the needs of culture. He never changed and yet he was always changing.

Sounds like a paradox to me.

This one may be the toughest paradox of all. Leaders will never reach a goal without being strong-willed. Without a stubborn will, obstacles will stop them. At the same time, they'd be naïve to think they have all the answers at the beginning of a venture. They must be open to voices of counsel; to flex and to adapt to changing realities. Duke basketball coach Mike Krzyzewski said it best: "The most incredibly interesting thing about being a leader is what adjustments you make and how you make them while keeping your core principles alive and well."

> The stubborn leader is like a mule, digging in his heels.
>
> The open-minded leader is like an octopus on roller skates.

To be clear, there are millions of stubborn, strong-willed leaders around the world that are not adaptable. They won't budge for any reason; they won't change their mind in the face of any argument. Their personality becomes good news and bad news for their teams. While they're predictable, ideas must be offered on the right day, and everyone must work around the will and ego of the leader.

Some leaders have just the opposite problem. There are truckloads of open-minded leaders whose teams feel like those leaders change their minds at the drop of a hat, based on the new trends that surface each year. I've spoken to employees who've said, "Yeah, we don't focus on one idea very long. Our boss is always into the newest fad." New programs. New ideas. New trends. You get the point. Teams consistently wonder who or what is the flavor of the month.

So, how do we embrace both a *strong will* and an *open mind*?

THE PARADOX IN REAL LIFE

Let's examine how this paradox showed up in Truett Cathy's life. I made a handful of observations on just how he balanced these two qualities that may seem like an oxymoron.

Truett determined what he was bullish about and unashamedly embraced it.

Dan Cathy, Truett's son and the current CEO of Chick-fil-A, told me, "In dealing with people, Dad was a study in contrast. He was very gracious, tolerant, and forgiving, but if you crossed a line, you knew it." Years ago, CFA executives met to discuss how the menu and ingredients in Chick-fil-A restaurants could be modified. Loads of ideas were suggested as they debated the topic, but after a long moment of silence, everyone looked down at end of the table to see Truett pondering the issue. When he looked up, he pointedly asked, "You're not changing my chicken sandwich, are you?" Enough said. That original chicken sandwich remains one of the top two selling products at Chick-fil-A every year.

When Truett was still running his first and only restaurant, the civil rights movement had formed in Atlanta and many restaurants were serving "whites only." It was common in the South. Since Truett wanted to serve all ethnicities, his African American customers would approach the side door and be served there, while white customers entered through the front door and enjoyed eating inside his Dwarf House. Over time, Truett felt hypocritical. So, he announced he wanted all customers to enter the front door and enjoy eating together. It was his own version of "integration." When blacks hesitantly entered, some white customers got up and left. Interestingly, Truett chased after them and said, "No. That's not how we do it here. You're going to come back and we're all going to eat in peace together." And they did. He was ahead of his time.

Truett's strong will usually centered on issues of quality, not quantity.

One of the iconic stories from Truett's leadership happened years ago. Boston Market, a direct competitor to Chick-fil-A, was growing quickly. The speed at which they were expanding caused a stir at the CFA Support Center. When executives compared the growth rate of Boston Market to theirs, they all felt the need to grow bigger, faster. After much conversation, however, they noticed Truett hadn't said anything. Everyone knew he wanted to grow, so it seemed odd that Truett was silent. When one of them asked for his thoughts, Truett replied with a Mark Twain sort of wisdom, "I'm tired of talking about getting bigger. I want to talk about getting better. Because if we're better, our customers will make sure we get bigger."

Another example of paradox is Truett's value of remaining closed on Sundays. Because Sundays are one of the highest revenue days of the week for quick-service restaurants, it seems like a contradiction to be closed and give that business away to competitors. But, alas, Truett was convinced everyone deserved a day of rest to be with their family and to enjoy a day of worship. One Tennessee Chick-fil-A operator couldn't resist the chance to make a sale and chose to open his restaurant on Sundays. When Truett heard about it, he personally drove up to the restaurant and fired the operator. The issue was clear to him. Did being a stickler for this value pay off? You tell me. The average McDonald's restaurant grosses about $2.6 million a year, open all seven days each week. The average Chick-fil-A restaurant grosses $4.2 million, open six days a week. Chick-fil-A makes more money per store each year than McDonald's, Starbucks, and Subway combined.[1] Truett's stubborn belief in being closed on Sundays also makes business sense: you attract more business when you care for your people and create scarcity.

Truett's open mind usually focused on expanding what he was bullish about.

Take the issue of money. Even though he was a billionaire, Truett still loved negotiating over a $5 difference in cost between rental cars on a trip. He loved negotiating the price of an antique car at an auction. Why? He cared about how he used his money. At the same time, however, he loved people, so he spent money to build a corporate headquarters with a five-story atrium and glass elevators in Atlanta. In one case, he'd scrutinize price tags, and in the other, he appeared to be careless. It's not true. He was frugal, but he wasn't cheap. He knew what he valued, and ultimately it was his people. He was open to spend money on something he cared about deeply. He used money and loved people, not the other way around.

In the early days, Dan Cathy remembers his dad talking to Charlie, their night manager at the Dwarf Grill. He could tell something wasn't right with Charlie and Truett had put lots of trust in him. Later, Truett took Dan out to the parking lot at the Dwarf Grill and looked up toward the roof. He then asked his teenage son to climb a ladder to see what was up there. When Dan climbed up, he found dozens of empty beer cans. Charlie was an alcoholic and would toss his beer cans on the roof assuming no one would find them. Dan came down the ladder thinking, "Well, there goes Charlie." He later discovered Truett didn't fire Charlie. Instead, Truett personally drove him to AA meetings until Charlie found his way to sobriety. Charlie remained employed there until he retired. Truett Cathy believed in people and proved it by how much he gave to those who needed it. Truett taught a sixth-grade boys Sunday School class on Sundays and later gave college scholarships to the boys who needed them. Truett started the Winshape Foundation, which was all about kids and families. He put charity at the forefront of his business model early on, before it became common in the fast-food industry. Chick-fil-A has given over $75 million to education and charities since its founding, according to the company.[2]

His approach was built on the belief that he should never miss an opportunity.

While he was bullish about his core beliefs, he remained open-minded because of his ferocious conviction that opportunity was something you can't always *plan on* but that you must *capitalize on.* It often snuck up on you, and only adaptable, open-minded people can benefit. This insight explains how he invented his original chicken sandwich. In the early 1960s, Truett was running his Dwarf Grill, near the Atlanta airport. He'd thought about adding chicken to his menu, but it took too long to cook for his patrons who had to eat a quick lunch. A local poultry supplier had been tasked with creating a small, boneless chicken breast for airline meals but ended up with quite a few extra chicken breasts that didn't fit on the airline food tray. He offered them to Truett at a good price and this became an opportunity to test ways to serve it. He tried various ways and got customer feedback. One way was a lightly breaded chicken breast, with two pickles on a buttered, grilled bun. Everyone one said: "That's it!" It was a hit.[3]

During the 1982 fiscal year, Chick-fil-A was struggling during an economic downturn. It was a difficult time for most businesses. That year, CFA had spent a million dollars over their budget. The executive team chose to take a retreat and figure out what to do. When they arrived, Truett decided the first question they must ask is not "what" to do, but "why" they even existed. This challenging time was an opportunity that forced them to understand their "why" long before Simon Sinek taught us to do so. Believe it or not, this became the fire that ignited everyone. Their "why" wasn't about selling chicken at all. They came up with their corporate purpose statement, which reads: *To glorify God by being a faithful steward of all that's entrusted to us and to have a positive influence on all who come in contact with Chick-fil-A.* The following year, the staff worked with greater energy, sharper focus, and higher morale, and the revenue followed.

Truett believed it was possible to play both hardball and softball at once.

Too many leaders make a choice between playing hardball or softball. The choice between "hardball" (tough management that tries to force a better bottom line) and "softball" (kind management that hopes for a better bottom line) can be transcended by a third alternative, which is to be both tougher and kinder. Truett believed if he made the values of the company clear and embodied them regularly himself, he could serve people well within those boundaries. For Truett, every team member was more important than his or her job, but no team member was more important than the mission.

Which one of these observations could be your greatest takeaway?

Truett decided to build his restaurant chain on excellent service, not just good food. Many questioned this decision, assuming that people buy fast food for the speed, not the service. But Truett and his son Dan were convinced this was the right approach. They called it "second mile service." At the annual CFA Seminar one year, Truett introduced the phrase "It's my pleasure." While we all know Chick-fil-A by this small phrase today, it took nearly a decade to instill it in the company's language. Why? Truett didn't play "hardball" and demand it. He simply brought it up over and over and over each year, encouraging his operators and staff to utilize the phrase until, today, we recognize it as Chick-fil-A's norm.

Truett never let the business outgrow him.

Over time, this founder began to not only franchise his restaurant brand and menu, but he was gracious and willing to share decision-making. Truett assembled a group of trustworthy leaders, and once he found them, he gradually weaned himself from what he'd been adamant about holding onto years earlier. Those who knew him knew he was strong-willed and were amazed at how he overrode that will to make shifts that would benefit the future of the restaurant. Growth and improvement trumped his own preferences and weakness.

Dan Cathy told me, "I watched Dad grow with the business. He started at twenty-five years old after selling his car to have enough cash to build his first restaurant, and over time he built a multibillion-dollar business without ever allowing it to outgrow him." According to Dan, Truett never became an impediment to improving the brand or its growth.

Consider this. When Truett was ninety-two, he launched a new restaurant called Truett's Luau, a new restaurant just south of Atlanta. Nearly every piece of décor in the restaurant was chosen by Truett himself as a senior citizen. It's very different from a Chick-fil-A quick-service restaurant, decorated as if you are in Hawaii, complete with Hawaiian music and serving fresh vegetables, shrimp, Mahi Mahi, and other Polynesian foods.

THE CRUX OF THE ISSUE

The fact is—strong leaders earn their right to be followed by how responsive they are to the input of team members. It's not so much that they don't know what direction to take, but they believe the best idea should win, wherever it comes from. They know where they need to go, but also believe that by listening, people feel heard and take the journey together. The team owns the mission, along with the leader.

Michael Abrashoff was the Navy captain of the USS *Benfold* back in 1997. When he took command of the ship, it was the worst performing vessel in the Pacific Ocean. The departing captain was jeered and booed as he exited the ship. Sailors hated his "command and control" style. It was a power trip, not a leadership journey.

Michael knew he had to lead in a different way, and he did.

Abrashoff was clear and strong in his leadership—he told his sailors he wanted to become the "best damn ship in the Navy." So, the first act he performed was to meet with each of the 210 sailors one-on-one to get to know them and hear their ideas. Much of his leadership was built from the ideas he got from young men and women on board. For instance, one day as the crew was painting the ship, a young sailor asked Captain Abrashoff permission to speak freely. When he got the nod, the sailor asked him, "Sir, has the Navy ever heard of stainless steel?" When the captain looked puzzled, he continued. "The reason we have to paint the ship so often is because the nuts and bolts rust out. If we found hardware that didn't rust, we can spend more time in training." At the next port, Abrashoff sent a team on land, armed with a credit card to purchase stainless-steel bolts. Now, the entire Navy uses them.

Michael gave "shout-outs" to his sailors on the intercom when he used their ideas. They bought into his leadership and owned the mission. They started setting records at target practice. What was needed was a paradoxical combination of both clear direction and genuine responsiveness to others. After one year, Captain Abrashoff had turned his ship around. The USS *Benfold* went from last to first, winning the coveted Spokane Award, which is given to the top performing fleet in the Pacific Ocean.[4]

The lessons learned from both student leaders and a tough Navy captain?

- Being strong-willed means you've got a shot at reaching your goal.
- Being open-minded means you've got a shot at taking other leaders with you.

STRATEGIES TO PRACTICE THIS PARADOX

This balancing act is not easy. When leaders do practice it, however, they become uncommon and extremely attractive to other strong leaders. You will attract the best people when you master it.

Let me offer you five strategies below that I've gleaned from not only my best days of leadership, but from watching uncommon leaders embody them so well.

The first strategy is to lead by principle.

I began working for a principle-centered leader in 1983 when I joined the staff of John C. Maxwell. John made every decision from a belief in a timeless principle that guided his actions. Principles are the ideals or truths a leader has found to work in the moment and that lead to a better outcome. For example, John taught each one of us on his team that he could give us authority (by a position), but we'd have to earn our own influence. He would affirm us in pubic but confront us in private. He'd always err on the side of generosity. He would believe the best about people. He managed by objective instead of telling us how to do our jobs. You get the idea. The principles in John's bestselling book, *The 21 Irrefutable Laws of Leadership*, were all familiar to me before they were published because John had lived by them for years. The advantages to principle-centered leadership are many:

- You don't merely react to difficult situations as they arise.
- You become consistent, predictable, and reliable to your team.
- Your mind is freed to think about other pressing issues.
- You're able to make decisions faster because you have a compass.
- Your leadership can be reproduced in other team members.

When leaders lead by principles, those principles guide big decisions; if there is no principle at stake or none violated, the leader can be open-minded to input on new ideas or changes. In the end, uncommon leaders decide what they'll be stubborn about and they're flexible on almost everything else.

The second strategy is to make sure one of your principles is: always make it better.

One of my guiding principles that prevents me from becoming too stubborn is the rule: "Always make it better." As I age, I tend to become set in my ways; I've found what works and I want to stick to my guns. What keeps me open to new input is my commitment to always improving the systems, the products, and the results. This is one of our core values at Growing Leaders. It has driven us to expand our *Habitudes*® from the printed page to e-books on Kindle, then to an online platform, and later to an app on a portable device. Each of these expansions was hard, but I valued results more than methodology.

What are your handful of principles that guide your leadership?

I wish Eastman Kodak could say the same.

George Eastman invented "film." He wanted to democratize photographs. Up until then, if you wanted a picture taken you had to hire a professional photographer. Eastman wanted to make the process better. His company ruled that industry for years. In 1973 they commissioned a twenty-three-year-old employee named Steve Sasson to attempt to build an electronic camera using a charge couple device. In 1975, Steve invented the digital camera. Unfortunately, the current executives had adopted a finite mindset. They suppressed the development of this new technology for fear it would cannibalize their own current model. They knew times were changing but they didn't want to give up what they were to gain. They made millions of dollars giving up the patents for digital cameras to sustain their current products. In 2012, Kodak filed for bankruptcy.

The third strategy is to apply "the Bit Market" principle. One of my favorite *Habitudes®* is called: "the Bit Market." It's built on a simple story. On his first day on the job, the president of an electric drill company that sold both tools and drill bits met with his entire staff to get a status report. Each of his vice presidents boasted about the number of drill bits their company sold each year. They owned 60 percent of the drill bit market, so they were sure their future was bright. After their reports, the president stood up, smiled, and sobered them all by saying: "This is all fine and well today, but we're forgetting one important truth: there is no market for drill bits." As his team stared at him in silence, he proceeded to say: "The market is for holes. And the day someone comes up with a better way to make a hole, drill bits will be obsolete."

How much do you value "make it better" in your current mindset?

This team had fallen into the same trap most human beings fall into: we fall in love with our current product so much, we forget why people buy our product. The only reason people buy a metal piece called a drill bit is because they have a problem they need to solve: they need to make a hole in a piece of wood. If another company developed an affordable laser that made a hole in a piece of wood easier, wouldn't we stop buying drill bits? In the music industry, we've shifted from buying LPs, to cassette tapes, to CDs, and now it's Spotify or Apple Music. All of these mediums are "drill bits." Music is the hole. Uncommon leaders never confuse methods with mission. They separate programs and products from purpose. The truth is, effective leaders always practice three actions:

1. They keep their eye on the "hole," not the "drill bit."

2. They are always looking for new ways to make "holes."
3. They sell the "hole" to the stakeholders, not the "drill bits."

We must stop selling product *features* to customers and focus on *outcomes*. If outcomes are our focus, we'll be much better at being stubborn about the right things in the present and open about the right things in the future.

"As a startup, figure out the problem you are addressing, and the users," said Waze cofounder Uri Levine. "Fall in love with the problem, not the solution, and the rest will follow." Levine was obviously describing the optimal situation for leaders to remain open to new and better ideas. In one sense, then, the secret is to remain *stubborn* about the problem your team is attempting to solve, then *open-minded* to the best ideas anyone comes up with to solve it. Far too often, organizations do the opposite. They fall in love with an idea for a product, create it, then get stubborn about its superiority, even as the market changes. Eventually, great companies like Kodak, Sears, Yahoo, Polaroid, J. C. Penney, AOL, Motorola, and others fail to see any need to be open-minded until it's too late. Maybe they forgot to stay in love with the problem they were trying to solve in the first place.

What's your current "drill bit"? What's your hole? What problem are you solving?

The fourth strategy is to avoid winning Pyrrhic victories. This is another *Habitude*®. It is built off the historical tale of King Pyrrhus, who led forty thousand Greek soldiers in battle against forty thousand Romans. It was the Battle of Asculum. After weeks of fighting, King Pyrrhus brought in elephants and finally crushed the wall his enemy was using to shield themselves and he won the battle. Afterward, one of his captains said to him, "Congratulations on your victory, King Pyrrhus." But as he surveyed the losses of equipment, time, and men, the king replied, "One more such victory and I shall be lost." This leader's point, of course, was simple: he had spent so much winning the battle, he may have lost more than he won. This still happens today. Our wins can come at too great a cost. We can win a debate with a customer over why a shipment was late and end up losing that customer for life. We can win a battle at work with a colleague and lose a war. We can win an argument with our teenager or our spouse and take a loss in the relationship.

Have you won any "Pyrrhic victories" recently? Do you keep your ego in check?

Let's face it. One reason for our stubborn spirit is often ego. A strong will, as I've said, can work for us and against us. If our ego drives our will, trouble is sure to follow. Uncommon leaders refuse to win a "Pyrrhic victory." In the moment of decision, they ask themselves:

- Is the issue worth debating?
- What do I hope to accomplish by winning?
- What effect will it have on the relationship?
- What's my motive for winning? (Why do I want to win?)

Victories can be won at too great a cost. A strong will can do as much harm as good. I must ask myself in each context: Do I value the method or the result? Do I treasure the details of this project or the relationship? My answer will guide what to be stubborn about.

The fifth strategy is to remember the future belongs to the young.

When Truett Cathy bought his first restaurant, the world was beginning to change. The "baby boom" had begun. The world was expanding, shifting, even morphing into something different. A few decades into his career, Mr. Cathy realized that some of his best ideas may come from other leaders, younger than he was. This enabled a strong-willed leader to be open-minded. Perhaps anthropologist Margaret Mead said it best in her 1970 book, *Culture and Commitment*, when she prophetically saw the future and gave a stunning explanation for how culture was transforming in a new era. Mead suggested human history can be divided into three eras:

1. **The Post-figurative Era.** This took place millenia ago when life didn't change much. Most people worked the same routines their grandparents did, embracing the same customs and traditions. The emerging generations during this period learned everything about life from the adults. Older generations all but dictated the youth experience. Your parents usually chose the person you'd marry. (Good luck with that.) Your career was usually the same as your father (if you were a son) or your mother (if you were a daughter), and your role was to perpetuate the cultural norms year after year, decade after decade.
2. **The Co-figurative Era.** This era began with the dawn of the enlightenment and the industrial revolution. At this point, cultural norms were changing; information could be obtained by anyone if they could read the printed page. Now the established adult and the emerging adult

figured out life together. At this point, youth had a say in the choice of marriage partners or what career path they chose, and even what worldview they embraced. This era lasted for centuries, right up to our lifetime. Both the old and the young had a voice in what the future held.

3. **The Pre-figurative Era.** Even fifty years ago, Margaret Mead could envision the day we'd be entering today. Smart technology, artificial intelligence, and the ubiquity of portable devices are shifting our world faster than ever. Not just incremental shifts but fundamental shifts are taking place, leading to a world where the young will figure out where life is going faster than the senior generations. Already, young people intuitively understand technology faster than I do; kids frequently maneuver through phone apps or tablets and seem to know where commerce is going. They're growing up in a "pre-figurative" world.

Where have you seen evidence that the future belongs to younger generations?

In the "Land of Tomorrow," young people are the "natives," and we are the "immigrants."

Because we're moving into a world where the young will be comfortable with new realities faster than the old are, it prompts me to listen to the natives and stay open-minded. Just remember, however, that if we're going to be open-minded leaders, we must possess both emotional security and a strong will. We must be emotionally secure enough to digest contrary ideas and strong willed enough to not merely swallow every novel idea just because it's new.

Summary of this paradox

WHEN I AM STUBBORN	WHEN I AM OPEN-MINDED
1. My team witnesses my tenacity.	1. My team witnesses my teachability.
2. People see I can stick to my decisions.	2. People see I can accept others' ideas.
3. I am viewed as a leader with convictions.	3. I am viewed as a leader who is adaptable.
4. Obstacles will not get in my way.	4. Opportunities will not be missed.
5. Others know what's important to me.	5. Others know that mission trumps method.

Practicing the paradox of being a strong-willed yet open-minded leader

1. When you're feeling stubborn, think of your "worst" and their "best." Picture yourself on your worst day and the other person on their best day. This enables me to stay open, to welcome contrary points of view, and to keep learning even from younger staff.
2. Start sentences with: "I'd be interested to know . . ." or with "Yes, and . . ." instead of "Yeah, but . . ." or "Let me give you context for that decision . . ." Use language that enables you to make your point but invite others' input. It is vocabulary that keeps the volley going instead of shutting interaction down. It has to be safe.
3. Rotate staff through your leadership team meetings. Allow team members who'd rarely get a seat at the table to have a seat, to listen in, then invite them to speak to the issues. While they may

feel intimidated, you'll be amazed at what you'll glean from their input.

4. Practice reverse mentoring. I mentioned this earlier in the book and will talk more about it later. Make a habit of meeting with someone from a different generation to mentor and be mentored. Focus on giving from your strengths and receiving from their strengths. Everyone can benefit from the story of a team member who's different.
5. Launch an exercise with your team: *Start, Stop, and Keep Doing*. Annually, leaders can meet with their teams to hear what teammates want them to begin doing, what they want them to stop doing, and what is it they do that they should continue.

As I reflect on Truett Cathy's leadership, almost everything he was bullish about concerned people. Methods, strategies, and techniques will come and go at Chick-fil-A, but the priority has always been to take care of their people, so their people can take care of their customers.

Early on, a high schooler named Eddie White worked for Truett at the Dwarf House restaurant. Eddie was a young black teen trying to make ends meet and help his family, who was financially challenged. During his junior year, Eddie wanted to take his girlfriend to the prom but had no car. Truett found out and gave him the keys to his car, insisting that Eddie use it. During Eddie's senior year, he dreamed of going to college, but didn't have the money to do so. Truett told him, "I want you to set a jar next to the cash register for people to make donations toward your college fund. I'll encourage everyone who can to contribute. Let's see what happens." When the tuition deadline came, Truett knew how much Eddie needed. He discovered what the donation jar still lacked, and surprised Eddie by making up the difference. Truett said, "Looks like you made your goal."

Truett continued this focus at corporate headquarters. People were everything to him. Well past retirement age, Truett kept a strict head count on the number of people on staff because he never wanted to have to lay people off in difficult economic times. Truett told his team that, regardless of what he was doing, if any guests asked to see him, he'd stop what he was doing to greet them. As a rule, he'd leave a meeting and graciously meet anyone.

Did this focus on people pay off?

I believe so. Truett's spirit was contagious. The speed, the service, the smiles, and the efficiency at most Chick-fil-A restaurants have expanded over the last two decades, many adding a second drive-through lane to the property. During the 2020 COVID-19 pandemic, drive-through service was all fast-food restaurants could offer customers—and Chick-fil-A absolutely benefited. I waited in long lines of cars to get my lunch, and later discovered that some of their restaurants set sales records during the "shelter in place" quarantine. They were ready for such a time.

It all began with a leader who modeled what it looked like to be strong willed and open-minded.

THINK IT THROUGH, TALK IT OVER

- Do you know leaders who are both strong willed and open-minded?
- What problems are you stubborn about solving? Does this keep you open-minded?
- Which do you struggle with more in your leadership: a strong will or an open mind?
- From the strategies covered, which might be helpful for you to expand upon?
- How could you improve on practicing this paradox?

PARADOX 5

Uncommon Leaders Are Both Deeply Personal and Inherently Collective

I was scheduled to meet her in November of 1997. But, alas, it was not to be. Our team traveled to several cities in India to teach leadership that fall, and had planned a meeting with Agnes Bojaxhiu, originally from Albania, but now living and working in Calcutta, India. Agnes changed her name once she took her Catholic vows, adopting the name "Therese de Lisieux," from the patron saint of missionaries. We know her affectionately as Mother Teresa. She passed away on September 5, 1997, less than three months before we'd hoped to visit with her. She was later honored in 2016 by the Catholic Church as Saint Teresa. She's been called the "saint of the gutters."

I perceived her as a saint long before she passed away.

Although Teresa was an educator for nearly twenty years, she became increasingly disturbed by the poverty in Calcutta. In response, she launched her own simple mission to the poor and dying on the streets of that city. I don't know that she had a strategic plan for scaling her work, but by 2012, her mission had over 4,500 nuns serving in 133 nations. It's the largest order of its kind and a legacy that outlives her to this day.

When she left her post as an educator to begin her own order, she attracted other young nuns, one by one, who wanted to join her in a very uncomfortable mission to the poor, the lepers, the sick (with tuberculosis), and the lame. Although her demeanor was quiet and unassuming, she was magnetic. Over the years, new branches of her congregation were created, including the Missionary Brothers of Charities, the International Association of Co-Workers of Mother Teresa, the Missionaries of Charity Contemplative Sisters, the Missionaries of Charity Contemplative Brothers, and the Missionaries of Charity Fathers.[1]

She envisioned serving as many marginalized people as she could during her lifetime.

She maintained such a big-picture vision for the task at hand that she didn't count how many needy people she served. Instead, she counted how many people were left to be served. She said, "I do not add up. I only subtract from the total number of poor and dying. With children one dollar saves a life. . . . So, we use ourselves to save what we can."[2]

Herein lies her secret.

When Mother Teresa was criticized for not being efficient with her systems or time, she tried to explain that her approach was what made it all work. Many asked: Couldn't government agencies, with their vast resources, do a better job serving the poor than a congregation of nuns? To this question she'd respond that God required her to do small things with great love, and that while government welfare programs exist for quite admirable purposes, "Christian love is for one person."[3]

Truth be told, because Mother Teresa remained close to the personal work of caring for sick and dying individuals, it furnished her with the gumption to take bold steps to fund the entire work. Once when she heard a large corporation in India was relocating to a new property, she set an appointment to visit the CEO and boldly asked him, "Would you like to do something beautiful for God?" When the executive smiled and inquired what she meant, she told him there were some "individuals who desperately needed his help." She ended up negotiating the donation of the company property to her mission. I believe courageous requests like this originated from staying personally close to the needs of her "clients."

The fact is that while our organizations may be about very different missions, we would do well to take note of Mother Teresa's style of leadership. What made her so effective and what enabled her to grow and scale in such an organic way is that she maintained her personal touch with everyone she served. As far as I could tell from my research, no one felt like a number. Not her staff, not her volunteers, and certainly not the recipients of her care. In short, as she grew The Missionaries of Charity into the largest order of its kind, she never lost the motivation that drew her into the work in the first place. *It was one life at a time.*

One of the most memorable illustrations of this was the day a group of business investors visited the Mother House and observed her washing the body of an older man with leprosy. When one of the observers scoffed and said, "I wouldn't do that for a million dollars," Teresa looked up at him and replied with a smile, "Neither would I."

"Mother Teresa visited the children's home herself each day, taking particular interest in the babies whose health was so precarious that they were likely to die soon. Wrapping the child in a blanket, she would hand him to a helper and simply instruct her to love the child until he died. She felt it absolutely central to her mission that no child should die without having experienced love."[4]

On the surface, we might assume practicing this kind of obsessive attention to detail will *destine an organization to fail,* but in fact, *it destines the organization to scale.* We intuitively know this is how life should be, and when we see it, we want to join it. Teresa wasn't into addition. She was into multiplication. She knew that by focusing on one, she was able to reach many. Her mantra could be summarized this way: *More time with less people equals greater overall impact.*

This becomes especially essential for leaders in times of crisis.

RESPONDING TO CATASTROPHE

Most of us will never forget September 11, 2001. The events of this fateful day took place almost exactly four years after Mother Teresa died. One of my most vivid memories was observing New York mayor Rudy Giuliani in the aftermath. Following the terrorist attacks, Giuliani coordinated the response of each city department while simultaneously organizing state and federal authorities for the World Trade Center site. Reports said he instantly synchronized citywide anti-terrorist measures and began discussions for the restoration of the destroyed infrastructure. For weeks, Rudy Giuliani made frequent appearances on television and radio providing updates on their progress, informing citizens what city tunnels would be closed as a precautionary measure, and where people could find help locating loved ones.

Some believe Giuliani acted out of his natural intuition. Others believe he was leveraging the opportunity for his own political gain. Still others believe he was doing what any effective leader would do. Whatever his reasons—Rudy Giuliani gave us a clinic on leading during times of tragedy, hardship, discouragement, and crisis.

In such times, leaders must find unique ways to practice both the *personal* and the *collective.*

For Mayor Giuliani, the days and weeks following the horrifying terrorist attack required him to continue clarifying his proposals on television, so every citizen could hear and grasp the game plan for restoration. He covered the "collective" through multiple appearances in the media, on TV, radio, and even written content on the internet. He leveraged every medium he knew of to reach every person who needed clear information. Simultaneously, however, Giuliani was attending funerals and memorial services, often multiple times a day, displaying a human and "personal" touch to his leadership. This, too, was broadcast on television. In interviews afterward he expressed condolences, explaining the contribution of the person who'd just been buried. It was as if he were a chaplain.

Both Mother Teresa and Rudy Giuliani were effective because they practiced a paradox.

THE PARADOX OF COLLECTIVE AND PERSONAL

People expect more from a leader today, especially during times of hardship. In one sense, the leader becomes much more of a public figure or representative of the people. One who speaks for them, feels with them, and offers a wise response in that context. People need big-picture vision from their leader, someone who grasps the gravity of what's happened, and the steps required to respond to it. At the same time, people need a leader who empathizes with their personal journey; someone who understands how the struggle feels to individuals, and who articulates the vision with a personal touch.

This is also true in everyday life.

Ours is a day of customization. People expect things to feel personal and created just for them—even positions on a team. Uncommon leaders find a way to tailor roles and tasks for individuals, while at the same time keeping the larger picture in mind and ensuring each person's talent is leveraged for the whole. These leaders somehow balance a *telescope* and a *microscope.* They see far and wide and grasp the whole, yet they see and care about the details and how those details affect the single mom who serves on the team. Peter Senge said it first: "Great leaders are inherently collective, and yet deeply personal."

So, how does this look? Here are some examples:

- This leader offers both professional training (which benefits the organization) and personal development (which benefits the individual). Everyone wins.
- This leader stewards the mission of the organization (or team), and at the same time, stewards each individual team member's time and talent.
- This leader can speak to the entire team, offering the big picture to them as well as offering personal examples of those who embody the vision from the lives of team members.
- This leader believes that no job is more important than the person, but no person is more important than the mission.

PARADOXICAL LEADERSHIP IN A PANDEMIC

Those who led a team during the coronavirus outbreak in 2020 saw how vital this balancing act is. As COVID-19 spread to the United States and other countries around the world, businesses, schools, and nonprofits were either shut down or their people were forced to work from home. Only essential retailers and first responders were still operating.

- Hundreds of millions were isolated.
- Tens of millions lost their jobs.
- Millions were infected.
- Hundreds of thousands lost their lives.

The times were so uncertain that anxiety levels rose measurably. Team members who continued working felt the angst of attempting to work in new conditions, utilizing technology in new ways, all the while wondering if their jobs were on the line. It was a sinister disease that methodically snuffed out normal life. It was surreal.

Our leadership team quickly discovered some fundamentals to lead well in such times. And it had everything to do with balancing the *collective* and the *personal.* Meetings with people and clear communication became even more important. The sequence of topics had to be:

1. **Personal items before business items.** If people know you care about their personal life, they'll feel secure enough to focus on the business. Talk about personal well-being, then the team, and then the overall mission. We had daily check-ins to discover how people were doing and to update them on our team progress. I inserted humor to relay I was still human and wasn't unsettled. Lastly, we offered our people a collective vantage point.
2. **Hard conversations before easy ones.** When it comes to news, I've found it's better to begin by handling the tough stuff, maybe even the negative updates, before you get into the easy or good news. Hard then easy. When we fail to do this, people can sense their leader is sugarcoating reality and may not trust what we're saying. When we practice "hard then easy" it displays strength and transparency on our part.
3. **Big picture before smaller details.** When we got to our discussion on the collective mission, I found

Which of these two—the collective or the personal—do you practice naturally?

> that providing the big picture allows anyone to place the details of their role into proper perspective. Give them the box top, then show where their puzzle piece fits. It really does work like putting a large jigsaw puzzle together. Box top first, then each piece. This prevents people from imagining an inaccurate narrative.

Most people know immunologist Anthony Fauci as the doctor at the forefront of the White House's response to the coronavirus pandemic. Dr Anthony Fauci, director of the National Institute of Allergy and Infectious Diseases, has practiced this paradox in front of our entire country, during the COVID-19 pandemic in 2020 and 2021.

"Fauci's political bosses—from Ronald Reagan to Donald Trump—have let him do the explaining because he is frank and understandable, translating complex medical information into everyday language while neither exaggerating nor downplaying," according to a news report on Al Jazeera. "Although he's spent his career in government, Fauci does not seem to have lost the human touch—and that may be part of the key to his success as a communicator."[5]

He spoke to the American public as a whole, offering updates on the COVID infections, how to best respond to them, the research on vaccinations, and what to expect in the months ahead. He is collective in his reporting. In the midst of that corporate communication, however, Dr. Fauci will often smile and speak to his listeners very personally, as if he's speaking to you as an individual, and remind you to wash your hands several times a day, to wear a mask, and to stay six feet apart when you interact with someone.

In 1990, when AIDS activists flooded the NIH to protest apparent government indifference, Fauci brought them to the table and met with them personally. He later helped to shape President Trump's initiative to end HIV in the United States.

During the 2014 Ebola outbreak, many Americans panicked when they heard a nurse was infected by a patient, a traveler from West Africa. Dr. Fauci responded to those fears by setting a personal example. After the hospital released that nurse, not only did he say she wasn't contagious, he gave her a hug on television to prove he wasn't concerned.

Collective then personal.

It only made sense. Leading any other way would have felt strange, inappropriate, and incomplete. To cover only the "collective" can leave teams feeling as if the leader doesn't understand their personal suffering. To cover only the "personal" may leave teams feeling understood but without a clear vision and plan for how to move forward. Teams need both empathy and clarity.

Many leaders struggle to lead their teams well in periods of angst. More than 6.6 million Americans filed for unemployment in one week during the pandemic. This was more than any single week during the Great Recession (2008) and felt more like the Great Depression (1929) according to people who lived during that time. New York City lost more people to the coronavirus than the city lost on September 11, 2001, during the terrorist attack. Dr. Anthony Fauci, from the White House Coronavirus Task Force, suggested we might never shake hands with anyone again. It was a strange time that required an "uncommon" leader.

A meme made its way around on social media during the outbreak that summarized what every leader needs to remember, as they lead during a crisis like a pandemic:

> We are all in the same boat—but we are not all in the same storm.
>
> For some people, it's sprinkling. This is a break. It's a breather. It's a rest. A time to reconnect with their families. Honestly, it's kind of peaceful.

> For some, it's a storm. It's a bit scary. It's disruptive. It's enough to make you stay up and watch the news and worry a bit.
>
> For some, it's a hurricane. It's tearing at the boards. It's pulling off the roof. It's washing them out to sea. It's dark and unknown. It is life changing.
>
> It's not wrong to be enjoying a sprinkle or enduring a storm. Rest with your family. But don't minimize the hurricane engulfing your neighbor. Laugh at a meme but get on your knees for those in the hurricane.

Our organization certainly experienced this storm, as we saw decreased revenue during this time of social distancing, but I know people who had it far worse. I know people who lost their jobs. I know some who were infected. I know several others who lost a friend.

What a strange time.

WHAT DO PEOPLE NEED MOST FROM THEIR LEADER?

Leaders must remember first and foremost that people under their care have different temperaments and will react to such times differently. People need three items most from their leader in tough times. As I both led and watched effective leaders during 2020, I saw a pattern. Wise leaders seemed to understand their people and offered them three gifts.

Context

It's easy for people to watch the news all day and get freaked out. They feel angst from all the bad news and the uncertainty of the season. Good leaders provide context to problems: this is not the worst crisis we have ever faced and yet it deserves our focused attention. Context means you furnish perspective on what's happening, you stay knowledgeable on current details, and you become a source of wisdom, especially for those who fall on either end of the spectrum: those who feel it's no big deal and those who feel like the sky is falling.

Applications

People usually need leaders to offer practical action steps during such times. It may sound silly, but sometimes grown adults need reminders of the applications they'd been given to respond to COVID-19: wash your hands many times a day, stay six feet apart from others, wear a mask outside, and shelter in place. The best leaders give people clear applications for their day. Clarity is the greatest gift a leader can offer their team in periods of uncertainty. We all live each day without certainty, but we can't live well without clarity.

Do you naturally follow this sequence when you lead in challenging times?

Belief

Napoleon Bonaparte said, "Leaders are dealers in hope." I believe we owe it to our people in uncertain times to offer belief and hope for a better future. This season will one day pass and we may just return to a better normal. I believe this. During the pandemic, Americans, once polarized in recent times, began cooperating and focused on helping each other. We were applauding healthcare professionals and first responders. Years ago, an experiment was conducted to discover how long a person could stand in a bucket of ice water, barefooted. The most profound outcome? Researchers found a person could endure the ice twice as long if someone stood next to them, encouraging them.

These three terms spell the word CAB. During the pandemic, I made a habit of regularly reminding myself I needed to take a CAB to reach the people whom I led during this period.

THE SOCIAL INTELLIGENCE OF UNCOMMON LEADERS

Lt. Colonel Christopher Hughes led a troop of soldiers in Iraq, during the second invasion. When a shipment of food, clothes, and blankets arrived from the United States for displaced people, Hughes felt the best place to distribute them was the local mosque. When he led his troops through the streets to meet with the cleric, local people saw them and assumed the worst. By the time Hughes and his soldiers arrived, the mosque was surrounded by locals with stones and sticks ready for a street fight. It was a huge misunderstanding. Fortunately, Hughes was a master leader. He first ordered his soldiers to halt. Then he asked them to point their weapons toward the ground. Next, he told them to take a knee, a position of vulnerability for anyone. Finally, he had his soldiers look up into the faces of the Iraqis . . . and smile.

One by one, the local people dropped their rocks and sticks. Slowly they became calm and began to smile back, long enough for Hughes to locate a soldier who spoke Kurdish and Iraqi Arabic to explain to them what they had in their packages and what their intent was.[6]

Disaster averted.

Lt. Colonel Hughes displayed what is called *social intelligence.* You may remember that I mentioned this subset of emotional intelligence in the first chapter. It's the capacity to navigate complex social relationships or environments. It's the very ingredient leaders desperately need today and what enables them to embody this paradox. Very often, relationships between different *generations* and *personalities* at work feel like "cross-cultural" relationships. When a Baby Boomer speaks to someone from Generation Z, both parties can feel like they are having a conversation with a foreigner who has different values, different customs, and a different language. Consider introverts and extroverts: when an extrovert explains how great it feels to talk to every single person at a party, an introvert can't identify with that at all. Each person feels like the other is from a different planet. The kind of effort that's needed to not only avoid damage but to foster collaboration is the same effort we must put into a relationship with someone from another country. And far too often, we're not ready to put in that effort.

If we're to embody this paradox, social intelligence is not a luxury, it's essential. The term was coined by E. L. Thorndike in 1920. According to researcher Daniela Wawra, "social intelligence is a necessary prerequisite for being a successful intercultural communicator."[7] Her summary of social intelligence includes:

- Social awareness (We're aware of how people are connected or disconnected)
- Attunement (We recognize others' emotions and actions via listening, observation)
- Synchronization (We accurately align our emotions to others as we communicate)
- Primal empathy (We feel what others feel, which informs our approach to them)
- Concern (We demonstrate genuine compassion and ascribe value to others)
- Self-presentation (We display a belief in others' potential and significance)
- Influence (We know how to wisely move people in a collaborative direction)

These skills obviously take practice to develop. At the same time, these qualities cannot be reduced to a list of behaviors that leaders tell their people to obey. We've all been greeted at a hotel or restaurant in a perfunctory way where we can tell the employee is only doing it because they've been told to do it. Customers today are too emotionally savvy for a trite greeting to have any meaning. *Emotional connections are the key, not behavioral modifications.* It's all about learning to read people before you lead people. I believe we must read, then heed, then lead.

WINNING THE STORY WARS

One of the chief benefits of being deeply personal yet inherently collective is what it does to the hearts of people. These paradoxical leaders garner an amazing brand in the minds of others. The narrative people carry about them is magnetic.

Do you evaluate another's emotional state before you communicate?

In the end, our success usually boils down to the "story" people carry inside them when they follow us. What do those team members believe about their leader that causes them to either do the bare minimum or go the extra mile? Whether they know it or not, leaders are constantly creating a story inside of their people, either positive or negative; personal or distant; trusting or avoiding. As a result, uncommon leaders recognize they are always shaping this narrative, both through their words and actions. It's a war of stories. These leaders win the hearts of their team by winning this war.

Jonas Sachs wrote a book in 2012 called *Winning the Story Wars.* It's all about how leaders form narratives inside people to motivate them toward a goal. Humans have always been obsessed with communicating. Throughout history, the stories we tell have defined us. But the way we've told them has also defined us. Effective leaders capitalize on the times in which they live and leverage the mediums available to them. Jonas Sachs believes humankind has experienced three major eras of communication.

Three eras of communication

1. **Oral Tradition Era**—An idea spreads from person to person, within a tribe. Everyone briefly owns it, modifies it, and can share it within their social network. Or, let it die. It was survival of the fittest and only the most compelling ideas lived and thrived because they were only verbally passed on. During this era, ideas felt personal but weren't scalable to large populations. The stories were communicated by mouth, person to person, family to family, community to community, but the process was slow and arduous.
2. **Broadcast Era**—Later, messages could spread via printed material and electronic media. Now, many ideas could be transmitted faster and wider to crowds the communicator didn't even know, because they could be recorded. Written language enabled us to copy parchments. The printing press enabled us to reproduce pamphlets and books. Electronics enable us to broadcast through radio and television and capture messages. A person could literally cast a message broadly. Now the message was scalable but not personal.
3. **"Digitoral" Era**—Today, a story or message can be relayed to a large number of people, but because it is done digitally (via computers and smart devices) it can once again feel personal and customized to a specific audience. Because it's digital, the message can be replicated and customized multiple times to many niches as if it were only for them. Now our communication and leadership can be both

> personal and scalable. Messages can be targeted at specific groups and sent out to specific audiences. The sky is the limit for leaders who leverage today's opportunities.[8]

Once again, however, it is survival of the fittest.

The key to leading in our time? Make progress toward number three as soon as you can:

1. Era One: Personal but not scalable.
2. Era Two: Scalable but not personal.
3. Era Three: Both scalable and personal.

If you're intentional, you can reach your largest audience, but still share a message that feels personal to everyone.

FIVE METAPHORS TO EMBRACE

Let's get practical. The remaining portion of the chapter, I'll attempt to lay out helpful ideas on how to practice this paradox—being both inherently collective and deeply personal. I mentioned earlier I love teaching leadership with images. I call them *Habitudes—Images That Form Leadership Habits and Attitudes.* Here are five of them below to guide you.

Windows and Mirrors. I believe when a leader pulls back the curtain and shares a window to their own soul, they offer a mirror for others to see their own. In other words, when you share your own personal struggles and humanity, people respect you more, not less. When you identify with others, it allows them to reflect on their own lives. Question: How could you improve on being authentic and transparent for your team?

Telescopes and Microscopes. I mentioned this one earlier. Effective leaders peer through a telescope to see far and wide.

They see the big picture. Yet they also utilize a microscope to see details and nuances in the lives of their team members. This deepens trust as people believe the leader sees future direction, but also understands how it affects the team. Question: How could you better communicate you see things both distant and detailed?

Which of these three do you capitalize on most? What could you do to improve leveraging the "digitoral" era in which we now live?

The Skinny Chef. When you enter a café at lunchtime, but notice the restaurant is empty and the chef is skinny—doesn't it make you question your decision on where to eat lunch? In the same way, people want to know their leaders are "eating" what they're feeding the team. Do they practice what they preach? This image reminds me my actions either confirm or damage my message. Question: How could you cultivate deeper credibility with your team?

Dentists and Cavities. Have you noticed when you get a cavity, your dentist wants to fill it as soon as possible? Why? Because dentists know if they don't fill it, bacteria will. In the same way, during times of uncertainty, people have mental "cavities," open spaces in their minds that can get filled with inaccurate narratives. Leaders must be dentists and fill those holes with truthful and accurate information. Question: How can you improve communicating collective and personal narratives for your team?

Stethoscopes and Treatments. No doctor greets a patient with a prescription in hand. They first perform a diagnosis before offering a treatment. Similarly, leaders must examine their people, holding a relational stethoscope to their hearts, before deciding how to treat them. Empathy should precede communication. Listen before you lead. Diagnosis comes before direction. Question: How can you better display a relational stethoscope with people?

Summary of this paradox

WHEN I AM COLLECTIVE	WHEN I AM PERSONAL
1. People recognize I see the big picture.	1. People recognize I see their story.
2. None are more important than the mission.	2. Each is more important than their job.
3. I provide professional training.	3. I provide personal development.
4. I steward the organization's mission.	4. I steward individual talent and energy.
5. I lead the whole team caring for the goal.	5. I lead individuals caring for their lives.

Practicing the paradox of an inherently collective yet deeply personal leader

1. **Do for one what you wish you could do for everyone.** My friend Andy Stanley liberated me with this challenge. Too often, leaders refrain from doing a favor for someone because they feel they can't do it for everyone. After all, it wouldn't be fair. In all honesty, this can be a cop-out. Instead, why not do some favor for a person who needs it, and let it be. Don't broadcast it and don't worry about the fact that you can't offer this wonderful gift to everyone on the team. Do this often enough, and you may just get around to everyone one day.
2. **Practice active listening before you say anything.** Native Americans once resolved conflict with a "talking stick." Two parties in conflict would sit down and only the one holding the stick could talk. Once they felt completely heard and understood, they'd pass it to the other party to voice their

perspective. Problems were solved this way. Social intelligence is developed when we actively listen without interrupting. We gain clues by hearing others' inflections, sensing nuances, and reflecting on what they meant. Taking notes is helpful.

3. **Be intentional to pay close attention to what's around you.** Observe your surroundings and the people who are close to you each day. Note the subtle social cues you receive from others and the cues people send to others around them. What messages are both sent and received? Notice the differences in how individuals interact with one person as opposed to another. You'll not only see that context explains conduct, but you'll learn how understanding others' contexts informs your own conduct. Your words will begin to be more personal.

Which of these six practices do you struggle with the most?

4. **Seek to add value to each person with whom you interact.** Because we are creatures of habit, I found I need to create good habits. One of mine this past year is this: if I have ten minutes or more in a personal interaction, I will do or say something that adds value to that person. I may share an idea or offer a word of encouragement or introduce them to someone I know who could help them or I recommend a book; you get the idea. When we interact with this mindset, our curiosity enables us to find personal connections.
5. **Pursue a new relationship connection every week.** This does something to our brains. Just as your bicep swells when you curl a heavy weight daily for weeks, your brain has plasticity and grows stronger

when you make personal connections with people. The neuro connections flow more efficiently in your brain. (Our skulls prevent our brains from swelling, but our transmitters can allow traffic to flow more efficiently when we develop connections with new people.) Cultivating new relationships is like a workout for your emotional intelligence.

6. **For each collective message you must offer, add a personal one that's relevant.** Leaders must never forget that people need both the collective and the personal. If your strength is displaying a very personal, even intimate style of leadership, you'll want to make sure you focus on portraying the collective and communicating the big-picture message. This week, be intentional about including both in your messages. Watch what it does to people, how it fills their cognitive and emotional tanks.

A PERSONAL GREETING CARD

It is one thing for a leader to follow through on the fundamentals of leadership. Effective leaders have followed protocol for centuries, even millennia. It is an entirely different thing for leaders to show up in a needed time and express thoughts that listeners feel are directed toward them, not just a crowd. They are real and relevant.

They combine the personal with the protocol.

It's like the feeling you might have when someone sends you a greeting card on your birthday but leaves no personal remarks on the inside of the card. The card was nice. Someone remembered you but it was the bare minimum. Hallmark® wrote the words, and this person just applied the stamp. The card takes on new meaning when the sender writes personal words of affirmation and best wishes. The sender goes beyond protocol and adds the personal.

Greeting cards were first used in ancient China and Egypt. Later, with the introduction of the printing press and postage stamps, greeting cards could be mass-produced. The earliest versions were simply a generic greeting, printed in large numbers, with only the signature of the sender near the bottom. Over time, traditions evolved and senders added their personal thoughts or feelings to the receiver on the card. In the same way, expectations for leaders have risen. Generic leaders are average leaders. They have the sense to be present, to show up when needed, offering a cue that the people there were worth their time. Again, however, this is the bare minimum, deserving an average grade. Their bodies are in the room. They "mailed a greeting card."

Effective leaders like Mother Teresa not only show up—but add their personal remarks to the bottom of their "greeting card." Even while still an educator, she kept a growing school personal as enrollment increased and admission became intimidating to new pupils. One of Mother Teresa's former students recalled, "I was a little nervous since I hadn't been to the city before and didn't know what to expect in this new school [St. Mary's, Loreto]. All my fears melted away on meeting Mother. The day I joined school, Mother Teresa came into the parlor, called me by my name in such perfect Bengali, and greeted me in the Bengali way and language. What a welcome she gave me!" And she did this for all of her students, greeting them by name using their own customs and in their native language.

THINK IT THROUGH, TALK IT OVER

- Which do you naturally tend to be: a collective leader who sees and acts on the big picture, or a personal leader who sees one person at a time? Do you know why?

- What's the number one takeaway you picked up from Mother Teresa or any of the examples in this chapter?
- What do you think is the most important advantage to practicing this paradox in the aftermath of a pandemic?
- What do you struggle with most when it comes to embodying this paradox?
- How could you improve your leadership in light of this paradox?

PARADOX 6

Uncommon Leaders Are Both Teachers and Learners

When Angela Ahrendts accepted the offer to become the chief executive officer of Burberry in 2006, the luxury coat company's sales were in decline. They had been for years. Burberry had been around for 150 years, and while the British brand retained an elite reputation, it was a company known for its plaids, and for selling coats to rich, older women.

Angela was asked to come lead the company because of her past success and experience. No doubt, she arrived on the scene with ideas for turning that company around. Which made her early moves curious. After meeting her direct reports, she scheduled a series of meetings with her youngest team members at Burberry. Beyond that she began recruiting sharp, young professionals, even interns, that she could meet with and listen to for insights into reaching millennials (a population Burberry was failing to reach at the time). "Ahrendts also hired a young marketing team, most of whose members were under the age of 25. Burberry jumped onto Instagram, Pinterest, and Twitter, using bold photography to engage millennials on their own turf."[1]

Probably the wisest move Angela made was to establish an in-house digital team led by a young Christopher Bailey (now Burberry's CEO), who served as chief creative officer, and John Douglas, who served as the chief technology officer. This team brainstormed ideas to attract young shoppers. One of the team's most successful moves was to launch "a new website and innovative social media campaigns, including the *Art of the Trench,* a photo platform that allows visitors to upload photos of themselves in iconic Burberry trench coats."[2] And boy, did those millennials post photos. Tons of them. I've been to the page on their site and it is full of pictures of young, classy, twenty- and thirtysomethings wearing Burberry coats on downtown streets.

In the end, it paid off big-time. In her seven years at Burberry, Angela raised the company's value from two billion pounds annually to more than seven billion.

What I love most about her story is that Angela entered as both a *teacher* and a *learner.* She was an instructor to her executive team, insisting they make moves to go digital, update their marketing approach, and hire young team members. Indeed, she put on a clinic in how to turn a brand around. Yet, among her wisest decisions was to become a student as well. One of her ongoing steps during her years at Burberry was to listen to young staff who intuitively knew how to reach their peers.[3]

Angela Ahrendts remained teachable as she moved into her next role as senior VP of Retail at Apple in 2014. In a report by *Business Insider,* we read, "Working in a senior leadership role at a technology company like Apple also showed Ahrendts the importance of moving quickly, especially in an age during which our attention is dominated by apps like Instagram, YouTube, and Uber." "I told the leaders very early on, move fast, fast," she said. "So, we got rid of all the manuals, got rid of everything and started doing 3-minute YouTube videos. That's how we united and aligned 70,000 people around the world."[4]

She was an instructor and a student simultaneously.

UNCOMMON LEADERS ARE TEACHERS AND LEARNERS

In our day of unceasing change, leaders are forced to be teachers, and organizations are forced to adapt. Michael Josephson said, "Great leaders are teachers, not tyrants. They help their followers see and understand more. They inspire them to become more and motivate them to do more." To do this, however, these leaders must first and foremost be lifelong learners, always adapting and never resting on what they know. Leaders are both receptacles of information and libraries of information. At least that's true of uncommon leaders.

The fact is, innovative products and services are launched every year by people who see an opportunity that others miss. The better we can leverage this "rookie advantage," the more we'll succeed in today's competitive world, just like Angela Ahrendts. Angela turned conventional wisdom on its ear: instead of executives coming up with ideas and then telling interns to implement them, the youngest on the team were brainstorming and the executives (with their network and budget) took the lead on implementation. Although Angela had great experience:

- She entered her role like a rookie.
- She remained teachable with less experienced team members.
- She was humble and hungry in her approach.
- She didn't rest on her laurels.

The wisest and most uncommon leaders remain in this posture their entire career. Late in his life, Walt Disney (whom we will examine later in this book) enjoyed telling a story to explain his job: "I was stumped one day when a little boy asked,

'Do you draw Mickey Mouse?' I had to admit that I did not draw anymore. 'Then, do you think up all the jokes and ideas?' 'No,' I said, 'I don't do that.' Finally, he looked at me and said, 'Mr. Disney, then what do you do?' 'Well,' I said, 'sometimes I think of myself as a little bee. I go from one area of the studio to another and gather pollen and sort of stimulate everybody. I guess that's the job I do.'"[5]

Which column would your team members say you embody most often?

Once again, a learner and a teacher.

Sixty years ago, President John F. Kennedy wisely mused, "Leadership and learning are indispensable to each other." This was never truer than it is today. Jay Samit said, "Lifelong learning is no longer a luxury, but a necessity for employment."

THE PARADOX AT A PODIUM

I remember watching Steve Jobs give the commencement speech at Stanford University in 2005. The place was packed. I am not sure what everyone expected to hear that day, but I can imagine. Perhaps Jobs might unveil a new Apple product; maybe he'd make a prediction for the future of technology. Perhaps he'd reflect on his accomplishments at Apple.

Instead, he surprised everyone.

He stood at the podium for fifteen minutes. And in that short time, he simply shared three personal struggles and the lessons he'd learned from them.

1. He spoke about how he'd never graduated from college himself. (There he was speaking at the prestigious Stanford graduation ceremony.)
2. He spoke about how he'd gotten fired from the company he had started. (Apple let their founder

go about a decade after he'd launched the organization.)

3. He spoke about how he had cancer and would die from it (probably soon).

When he finished and sat down, the crowd roared and gave him a standing ovation.

What I appreciate most about this speech is that Steve became vulnerable. This legendary leader, this influential icon became human again. Steve Jobs metaphorically stepped down from his pedestal while he was standing at the podium. Suddenly, the playing field felt level. Everyone was learning. This is very tricky as teachers and learners seem to possess two different mindsets. One feels like a master of knowledge, while the other feels like a protégé, a consumer of knowledge.

In reality, teachers and learners can embrace a similar paradigm as long as teachers see themselves as a fluid receptacle of content, always dispensing yet always consuming. Every time I teach an audience (including my own team), I tell myself: "This is what I know today . . ." I'll often say to the people to whom I am speaking: *This is what I know today, but I know there's more to know.* Our learning is dynamic and limitless. This allows my delivery to be confident and passionate, while at the same time hungry and open to learning from my listeners in a Q-and-A session. It requires an intentional decision.

This posture of learning is a popular one among some of the most accomplished people in history. Brian Herbert once explained, "The capacity to learn is a gift. The ability to learn is a skill. The willingness to learn is a choice." The greatest "masters" throughout history agree. Michelangelo said, "I'm still learning" when he was eighty-seven years old. When legendary cellist Pablo Casals was asked why he continued to practice at age ninety, he replied, "Because I think I'm making progress." Even Mahatma

Gandhi once said, "Live as if you will die tomorrow. Learn as if you will live forever."

IDEAS FOR BECOMING A LEARNING LEADER

The first step toward becoming a learning leader: managing emotions

The prerequisite for remaining a learner while you are a teacher is emotional security. If you're an insecure leader, you'll soon begin defending your past ideas; you'll feel threatened or even displaced if someone has a better solution than yours. To preserve your own "turf," you'll stop listening to others. I have watched teacher-leaders become embarrassed and humiliated when a team member offers a better insight to the conversation. When their ideas are challenged, they reveal their true colors, becoming defensive, irrational, and even emotional. Why is this? When your competence is challenged, your amygdala lights up inside your brain, and you shift into fight or flight mode, rather than relying on the rational part of your brain. You spiral into survival mode, preoccupied with how you appear to others rather than securing the best idea, regardless of who it comes from. Soon, you'll feel the need to dig your heels in and "stick to your guns" when people question you. Frankly, I do not know one teachable leader who isn't also an emotionally secure person. This step is all about growing your emotional intelligence.

Remaining a learner when you've got the role of a leader and teacher requires management of our emotions. It demands we master the first two of the four competencies that define emotional intelligence:

1. Self-awareness
2. Self-management
3. Social awareness

4. Relationship management

The first two from this list require personal development. They're about becoming cognizant of the emotions we feel in any given moment, what triggered them, and how to manage a response that enables progress. The second two are about translating those concepts into our social interactions. Emotions always serve a purpose, and because they are reactions to your life experience, emotions always come from somewhere. What makes staying in a posture of "learner" when you're a seasoned veteran extra challenging is that some of our lessons will come from others with far less experience, and perhaps of even lower intelligence and competence.

This, however, is what uncommon leaders do.

My daughter Bethany got a jury summons when she was eighteen years old. It was a store robbery and murder trial, which was quite a traumatic experience for a teen. Both attorneys wanted her on the jury, assuming she'd be easy to persuade. (She was clearly the youngest and least experienced person in the courtroom.) The prosecutor and defense made their cases, and the verdict was left to the jury who deliberated for hours. At one point, it was a hung jury. Bethany remained quiet and respectful. Finally, when one juror asked what she thought, she posed a question: "Have you all noticed the nervous habit the defendant has of playing with his shirt collar while he's on the witness stand?" When everyone nodded, she suggested they watch the surveillance video of the robbery again. Sure enough, the man robbing the store played with his collar in the exact same way. Soon, the jury was clear, and the verdict was rendered. After it was over, the judge approached her, saying, "Young lady, you are very observant. I knew more than what I was permitted to share in this trial. I'm just glad someone like you was discerning enough to pick up on the cues."

I'm sure the victim's family was also glad the jury listened to a teen with less experience but a high emotional intelligence. Bethany told me later it was anguishing because she felt empathy for both the victim's and the defendant's families; both now had lost a family member. She was able, however, to sift through her emotions and make a tough decision. This is what emotional intelligence achieves.

People with higher emotional intelligence (the ability to manage emotions in any situation) make more money (about $29,000 more a year) than those with low EQ (emotional intelligence) and rise to higher positions as well.[6] In most industries, the higher your position, the greater the need for high EQ. I believe one of the clearest tests of your emotional intelligence is staying teachable (even with underlings) as you rise in prominence. Relationship management is your ability to use your awareness of your own emotions and those of others to manage interactions successfully.

I got a clinic on this topic from John Maxwell almost forty years ago, when I first joined his team. John became senior pastor of Skyline Church in San Diego in 1981, following the founding pastor, Orval Butcher, who'd been there twenty-seven years. When John arrived, he noticed an older gentleman named Harry didn't seem to like him or his leadership style. Harry and his wife attended on Sunday mornings, but Harry would hardly respond when John greeted him, and wouldn't shake John's hand when he extended it. Finally, John asked Harry's wife if something was wrong. John wondered if he'd offended him in some way. She smiled, saying, "No, you've done nothing wrong. It's just that Harry loved Pastor Butcher, and now—you're his replacement." The following week, John decided to risk asking Harry if they could meet briefly. Harry agreed and came to the office, sat down with his arms folded and a scowl on his face.

This wasn't going to be a congenial meeting.

John sat across from Harry and thanked him for coming in. Then, John surprised him by asking, "Would you mind sharing some of your favorite memories of Orval Butcher?" Harry lit up. He began sharing fond recollections from over the years—how Orval had married, buried, and baptized many of his family members. When he finished, John leaned forward and responded, "Harry, those are great memories. I can tell you really appreciate Pastor Butcher. And for whatever it's worth, I think you should keep loving Orval the way you do right now. He was a great leader and friend." Harry was a bit surprised by this disarming encouragement. After reflecting a moment, John simply added, "But, Harry, after you love Pastor Butcher with all that love . . . if there's any love left over, could I have it?"

Harry was stunned. All his new leader was asking for was the allegiance he was able to give. Both men teared up that day and, for the first time, Harry offered John a hug on his way out. Following this meeting, Harry was seen smiling again and even returned to some of his past activities around the church, leaving everyone wondering: *What's happened to Harry?* What I recall most vividly is that Harry would linger after Sunday worship services each week until almost everyone else was gone. He would sneak up on John Maxwell, give him a big bear hug, and whisper in his ear: "This is the love I got left over."

The bottom line? John Maxwell managed his emotions for the sake of someone else. Most of us would agree that solid relationships are something that should be sought and cherished. They are the result of how you understand people, how you treat them, and the history you have. The equation is logical and easy to understand:

- When you manage your own emotions, you tend to have better relationships.
- When you have better relationships, you tend to be open to what others say.
- When you're open to what others say, you remain teachable and keep growing.

The second step toward becoming a learning leader: putting paradigms to work for you

As you likely know, paradigms can be your best friend and your worst enemy. A paradigm is a set of rules that define boundaries and tell you how to succeed within those boundaries. Our brains naturally develop these frameworks, so we don't have to consciously think about everything we do during the day. How much of our day is habitual? Studies by neurobiologists and cognitive psychologists indicate that between 40 to 95 percent of human behavior—how we think, what we say, and what we do—falls into the subconscious category. Even if it's only 50 percent, we are on autopilot half the time—brushing our teeth, driving on the right-hand side of the road, grabbing that first cup of coffee each day.[7] If we did not possess paradigms, we'd be exhausted by noon, using up mental energy for each and every routine we do.

How well would your family and team members say you manage your emotions?

Our problem is—paradigms also limit what we can see. We miss some realities because we see things only through our accumulated lens. We stop offering good thought to many decisions and actions that deserve fresh thinking. At this point, leaders need a paradigm shift. A shift in paradigms occurs when our accumulated rules change. It's like changing the lens through which we see reality. Let me illustrate. Read this simple sentence below:

London in the the summertime.

Did you catch the fact that the word "the" is used twice in the sentence above? We often miss it because our paradigm for sentence structure assumes that we know what the phrase says. The second "the" doesn't belong there and we're used to reading sentences correctly. We may miss mistakes or overlook a new way of saying things. We may even ignore a glaring flaw that others can see. Our assumptions and expectations blind us in a bad way. The bottom line:

1. Paradigms create expectations.
2. Paradigms limit expectations.

I have benefited from this very reality.

I began formally creating the *Habitudes®* curriculum in 2002, right after neuroscience had made some amazing discoveries about the right and left hemispheres of our brain. I observed how the traditional pedagogies used in schools and training centers taught with lots of impressive words and very few pictures. After all, pictures don't feel scholarly or academic. History class was an exercise in memorizing dates, battles, and military generals. But our brains think in pictures. Our cerebral cortex retains information through images and our amygdala retains experiences via emotions. I thought: Why not harness the big idea I want to teach with an image that stirs both thought and emotion? That's exactly what our tool does. *Habitudes®* are images that form leadership habits and attitudes. Each image represents a timeless principle, and sparks both emotion and conversation since pictures are worth a thousand words.

I wasn't bound by past paradigms that traditional educators often are.

When you're a teacher and a learner, you can think more like a person outside of your industry.

You're more open to receiving all inputs, not just your own or those selected from a chosen few. Albert Einstein recognized this decades ago when he said, "I have no special talents. I am just passionately curious." *His hunger to learn trumped his library of knowledge.* He went on to say, "Once you stop learning you start dying."

The vital elements to make a paradigm shift are these:

- Begin with the end in mind, not with your current reality: What is it we want to achieve?
- Ask successful people outside of your industry: If you were me, what you would do?
- Walk out the door and return, imagining: If we were to start over, how would we do it?

In the fall of 2016, BlackBerry announced their plan to stop making smartphones. When I remember their beginnings, it's hard to believe. BlackBerry led the way almost twenty years ago, with their iconic mobile device, its QWERTY keypad, and its sophisticated software. At one point, they owned 50 percent of the market. In the end, that shrank to 1 percent. Sadly, when BlackBerry failed to anticipate primary changes in the market, iPhones and Androids took over. They failed to adapt to a new paradigm. They failed to listen and learn.

Alvin Toffler put it this way: "The illiterate of the future will not be those who cannot read or write. The illiterate of the future will be people who cannot learn, unlearn, and relearn. The question for us is, 'What have we learned that we need to unlearn?'"

The third step toward becoming a learning leader: avoid the Space Shuttle Defect

This is one of our newest leadership images. In January 1986, the Space Shuttle *Challenger* exploded seventy-three seconds into its mission, killing all seven people on board. Devastating. Sadly, we later learned the tragedy was caused by an error in the design that the engineers were aware of but did not redress.

In 2003, the Space Shuttle *Columbia* exploded while on its mission, again killing all seven on board. Foam insulation had broken off the launch vehicle on nearly every takeoff and NASA had gotten used to it. These foam pieces became projectiles that hit the underbelly of the shuttle. It happened so consistently on test flights that it became viewed as a normal consequence of the process—no harm, no foul. It turns out there was harm. This time, seven astronauts died.

Sometimes flaws become normal.

In both space shuttles, managers, scientists, and engineers at NASA stopped asking serious, rigorous questions about defects. NASA had quality control engineers who warned that the shuttles had defects, but they were ignored. The seemingly benign defect was not serious enough to warrant a costly redesign. The foam projectiles were simply seen as an unintended but regular part of the launch process.

Every organization experiences the normalization of defects. Our new president, Steve Moore, brought this to light when he joined our team. We began discussing examples of our failure to create efficient systems because we had become satisfied with "work-arounds." I've even had them in my personal life. Over the years, things go wrong with my car: a passenger door handle requires a jiggle to open it, a light on the dashboard won't go off, or a small noise under the hood won't go away, but I find a way to put up with it and get by.

How do you stay open to adopting new paradigms?

The fact is, every industry learns to tolerate recurring problems rather than fix them. It is part of the cost/benefit analysis that is done up and down the organizational hierarchy all the time. This willingness to expect, tolerate, and assimilate recurring problems in the workflow of an organization is technically referred to as the "normalization of defects."

Why do teams let this happen?

We normalize defects when we feel we're still able to function and fail to see the original methods we used may no longer be relevant. Consider the case study of the Space Shuttle *Columbia.* In his talk to our team, Steve Moore suggested people are tempted to tolerate recurring problems in normal operations in the following four scenarios:

1. We are still successful. *Columbia* flew its first mission in April 1981 and flew twenty-six other successful missions before the disaster occurred. The temptation leaders face is to accept suboptimal conditions so long as the overall results are acceptable. It seems "good enough."
2. The impact is tolerable. Once a defect has been normalized, the urgency to address it goes away. When it became clear *Columbia* was again struck by foam, several people within NASA pushed to get pictures of the breached wing in orbit. The Department of Defense was prepared to use its orbital cameras to get a closer look. Sadly, NASA officials declined the offer.
3. The work-around is doable. After a successful mission, the shuttle underwent routine maintenance lasting for months to prepare for a future launch. Repairs associated with pieces of foam striking the underbelly of the shuttle were part of the work-around.
4. The cost/benefit is acceptable. Quality control experts often ask the question, "Why do we have time to do it again, but we didn't have time to do it right the first time?" We convince ourselves that time repeatedly spent on a work-around is somehow better than investing a larger amount of energy to fix a problem long term.

HOW ORGANIZATIONS AND TEAMS EVOLVE

Reflect for a moment. One big reason we "normalize defects" regularly is because of the typical growth cycle. In his book *Managing Corporate Lifecycles,* Ichak Adizes describes the "Infant stage" where every organization begins its journey.[8] As you launch a new team or project, you often start with an idea you're excited about. Your team and mission are babies. You hope to survive. Next, you enter the "Go Go stage" where you begin to experience momentum. Your products or services are selling. You feel like a successful entrepreneur. In this stage, you gain viability and credibility among your peers—and you're forced to quickly come up with solutions to the problems that come with the volume and velocity of your progress. These solutions are not often long-term solutions, but quick fixes because you're living in the moment. You're not a baby anymore, but a toddler who's beginning to walk and run. The problem is—the systems you create often work in the moment but may not be the best systems for the long haul. As you move into the "Adolescent stage," new systems are usually required to scale. You must stop implementing "work-arounds," thinking things are "good enough." Leaders and teams must consistently:

- Update their products and services.
- Upgrade their process and systems.

Thankfully, the stakes associated with normalizing a defect are rarely as high as the *Columbia* or *Challenger* tragedies. But every team is vulnerable to *excellence fatigue,* where recurring problems that don't appear debilitating are eventually normalized. Leaders often fail to see their defects as problems to solve. They fail to upgrade and update.

SHIFTING PERSPECTIVE

Jack Welch taught me something years ago. Shortly after he took over General Electric as chairman and CEO in 1981, he met with his executives for an exercise. They listed all the products they sold—from blenders and toaster ovens, to stoves and refrigerators—and then they discussed their value to the company and customers. As they talked about each product, they asked themselves:

- Does this need a face-lift? (*It's good, but it just needs an update.*)
- Does this need an overhaul? (*Its purpose is good, but now it must be altered.*)
- Does this need a funeral? (*It once was good, but no longer is relevant.*)

General Electric decided they would only keep the products that could be number one or number two in the industry. Otherwise—change was in the wind. Did it work? You tell me. Under Jack Welch, GE's value increased by 4,000 percent.[9]

I believe every company, school, team, and family should conduct this exercise as they choose how to lead today. I want to challenge you to make your own list and have the same conversation in your organization: What would you change? What would you terminate?

The fourth step toward becoming a learning leader: make interruption introductions

I suggested this idea in the first chapter. The COVID-19 pandemic introduced new habits and attitudes into many categories of our lives. While millions saw it as one gigantic interruption, I'd like to suggest a better way to approach our "new normal." I read three futurists who recently compared today's pandemic to a new weather pattern. They described it as harsh weather we must learn to endure for quite some time. One of the authors, a social scientist, believed it is most helpful to describe our "new normal" with these metaphors:[10]

> **At first, we faced a Blizzard.** The quarantine lasted for months and its outcomes will continue to annoy most of us. It was like being hit with very bad weather that shut us all inside our homes. We watched and heard about victims of the coronavirus on television.
>
> **It is part of a longer Winter season.** The new normal we've entered will likely last one to two years (or more). Beginning in March of 2020, we began to hear doctors, scientists, and celebrities talk about bracing for a longer-term pattern that will force us to get used to a new lifestyle.
>
> **Which is all part of a new Ice Age.** Winter, of course, represents a shorter period than an era or "ice age." We're not certain about the specifics, but we may be entering a new era for the next four to six years. We'll interact differently, handle work differently, shop differently, and live differently for some time.

Where have you experienced the normalization of defects?

So, how do we manage this well?

The leaders I know who practice both teaching and learning have made a habit of perceiving interruptions as introductions. They're able to adapt to unplanned and often unwelcome shifts in their circumstances and leverage them as tools to help them on their way.

Consider the story of Uber Technologies.

Uber's story began in Paris in 2008. Two friends, Travis Kalanick and Garrett Camp, were attending LeWeb, an annual tech conference the *Economist* describes as "where revolutionaries gather to plot the future." Rumor has it that the concept for Uber was born one winter night during the conference when the pair was unable to get a cab. It was frustrating. Why was getting a ride from an event to their hotel so difficult? Their fast-paced day suddenly ground to a halt due to an antiquated taxi system. Yet it gave Travis and Garrett time to think. Initially, their idea was for a timeshare limo service that could be ordered on an app. After the conference, the entrepreneurs went their separate ways, but Camp continued to be fixated on the idea and bought the domain name Ubercab.com.

What's your natural response to interruptions? Have any enabled you to make progress?

Like so many other startups, Uber's idea really began when Travis and Garrett saw the entire system as antiquated while traditional cab companies continued doing business the way they always did it. These two gentlemen faced what many of us have faced—trying to increase their chances at getting a ride by standing in a more popular location (where cabs congregate), attempting to hail a cab yet being unable to for a long and uncertain period, and finally, not being sure of the cost of the ride once you got in the car all seemed like a "dinosaur model" to these entrepreneurs. Additionally, emerging technology made the old model totally unnecessary. Smartphones were becoming ubiquitous, apps were becoming familiar, and "on demand" reflexes were already taking root in the general population.

The ease and simplicity of ordering a car fueled the app's rising popularity. With the tap of a button, a ride could be ordered, GPS identified the location, and the cost was automatically charged to the card on the user account. The features fit the times:

1. You find your ride on your phone and it comes to you.

2. You know exactly what the cost of your ride is up front.
3. You know the kind of car and driver's name ahead of time.
4. You can see former passengers' ratings of the driver's service.
5. You know the time it will take to get you to your desired location.
6. You exchange no cash at the time of your ride or exit; it's all online.
7. Your payment is less clumsy and is likely lower than a traditional taxicab.

What's not to like about this model, right? So why didn't traditional taxi companies shift to this new paradigm years earlier? After all, they already had the workforce and infrastructure. The answer is easy: they didn't see their model as an interruption to busy people. They stopped being learners. Since they're in the driver's seat, they likely never understood the challenges their customers faced. Uber is now a part of our twenty-first century "gig economy." While it isn't perfect, the idea was easy for a couple of guys outside of a traditional taxi company to see, when interrupted.

Summary of this paradox

COMMON LEADERS	UNCOMMON LEADERS
1. Listen to me when I speak.	1. Speak to me and I'll listen.
2. I know the answer already.	2. I am seeking new alternatives.
3. Never question my judgment.	3. Let's always be asking questions.
4. I seek solutions from experts.	4. I seek answers from anyone.
5. I want your respect.	5. I want your input.

6. This is the way we've always done it.	6. I am looking for ways to make it better.
7. I'll figure it out myself.	7. Let's collaborate and the best idea wins.
8. Never let them see you sweat.	8. I am authentic and vulnerable.
9. I have more experience, so I know best.	9. Since I am older, I'm working to adapt.
10. I am the only teacher on this team.	10. I am a lifelong learner.

Practicing the paradox of being a teacher and a learner

1. **Practice reverse mentoring across your leadership team.** This is essentially what Angela Ahrendts did when she joined Burberry. She met with those different than her (younger, different skill set, varied background) and sought their insight while she offered her insight. Why not match your seasoned veterans with your newest team members and have them swap stories? Then, allow them to spot where they could add value to the other and mutually coach each other. Every generation can learn from the others. Peter Drucker said, "The most pressing task is to teach people how to learn."
2. **Make it a weekly (or monthly) goal to learn something new.** Each January, I determine five to six areas in which I want to grow. They vary from financial investments, to cultivating a better marriage, to the art of negotiation. Next, I choose specific people who can mentor me in each area. I don't assume one person can be "Socrates" and coach me in all areas, just a specialist who's ahead

of me in one area. I meet with them regularly, bring a pad of questions, and seek to learn. What if you identified a team of specialist mentors who can coach you in your goals?

3. **Establish regular times for personal and professional growth in your team's calendar.** To use a cliché: too often we only spend time working in our business instead of on our business. I've improved my personal growth and my team's growth curve by planning times for learning and development. We meet at weekly team growth times; I host an optional monthly leadership session, then one-on-one coaching times, too. The key is to be intentional, just as we are with our meals. I had a mentor who used to ask me: *When was the last time you did something for the first time?* Good question. John Dewey put it this way: "Education is not a preparation for life. It is life itself."
4. **Each time you gain an insight, find someone with whom you can share it.** This can be a fun exercise. Every day, I learn something from someone, by reading, listening, or observing. Immediately, I grab my phone and write it down, then I look for a suitable person who may benefit from the insight, too, and I share it. This enables me to remember it, plus adds value to someone else and keeps them learning. Author T. D. Jakes put it this way: "The world is a university and everyone in it is a teacher. Make sure when you wake up in the morning you go to class."
5. **Each quarter, discuss work functions that need to apply *the Space Shuttle Defect*.** We discussed this concept earlier. Meet with your leadership team

and list the products you offer and the systems you use, then answer whether any of them need:

- A face-lift. (It's a relevant idea but needs to be updated in appearance.)
- An overhaul. (It was a good idea but now needs an upgrade in how it functions.)
- A funeral. (It used to be relevant years ago, but no longer serves its purpose.)

Then, begin scrutinizing your work-arounds. What have you endured that, if genuinely resolved or addressed (fixed, in other words), could accelerate progress?

Leaders who practice this learning and teaching paradox must remember:

- You can't always choose your classroom.
- You can't always choose your teacher.
- You can't even choose your lesson.

But if you're a teacher *and* a learner, you'll remain valuable the rest of your life.

THINK IT THROUGH, TALK IT OVER

- Do you know leaders who are both teachers and learners? Who are they?
- What traits do those leaders have in common?
- Which do you struggle with most: being a teacher or a learner? Why?
- From the five practices above, which could be most helpful to you?
- How could you improve on practicing this paradox?

PARADOX 7

Uncommon Leaders Model Both High Standards and Gracious Forgiveness

Different circumstances call for different kinds of leadership approaches. Franklin Roosevelt, for instance, was an electoral leader who had to be inclusive as he presided over Americans during the Great Depression and World War II. He led in a democracy. Other leaders reject the idea of a popular vote to achieve quite different objectives. They are radical. Their followers may be fewer, but those followers will be more intense. These radical leaders "are prophets to their admirers, and fanatics to their critics," writes author Garry Wills.[1]

- They are singularly focused.
- They refuse to be distracted by other issues.
- They are willing to fight to the end achieving a goal.
- They are impatient with anyone who's uncommitted.

- They're completely fine when less passionate people don't join.

This is exactly the kind of leader Amarintha Tubman was.

Though her colleagues called her Minty, Amarintha gave herself the name Harriet once she launched her leadership campaign. We came to know her as Harriet Tubman in our history books. She was born a slave in 1825, but escaped her bondage in Maryland to the North, and could have lived a peaceable life from that point on. But she wasn't satisfied with her personal freedom. She defied the odds again by returning to the South to gather other slaves before and during the American Civil War and to help them escape as well. She leveraged her "Underground Railroad" to lead bands of African Americans to their freedom from the atrocious bondage they endured.

A DIFFERENT STYLE OF LEADERSHIP

Harriet came to be known for her military commander style. Although she was a woman of color (a minority within a minority at the time), she had no trouble establishing her nonnegotiables and enforcing them with anyone who joined her "team." The characteristics below define Tubman's leadership style and differentiate it from other forms of leadership.

This kind of leader doesn't look for consensus, but forms consensus. Dr. Martin Luther King Jr. was famous for saying, "A genuine leader is not a searcher for consensus, but a molder of consensus." Leaders, he believed, don't look outward to see what folks want to vote for and then act; instead, they themselves have already voted with their life and seek those who'll join them. Margaret Thatcher explained, "To me, consensus seems to be the process of abandoning all beliefs, values, principles, and policies in search of something in which no one believes, but to which no one objects; the process of avoiding the very issues that have to be solved, merely because you cannot get agreement on the way ahead. What great cause would have been fought and won under the banner: 'I stand for consensus'?"

This kind of leader knows what's important and will not compromise on values. Tubman knew she had no chance of succeeding if she ran a slipshod operation. The cause was too important to give it a half-baked effort. Nothing short of excellence would do. People in general need a leader to convince them of what they're capable of doing. And that leader embodies a values-driven lifestyle that others want to emulate. Jon Stewart clarifies the potency of values, saying, "If you don't stick to your values when they're being tested, they are not values; they're hobbies." Values are strong guardrails that simplify choices and keep us on the right path.

This kind of leader cares less about being liked and more about being respected. Steve Jobs said, "Be a yardstick of quality. Some people aren't used to an environment where excellence is expected." One strength of this type of leader is that they care little about winning people over. They're in a productivity contest, not a popularity contest. This is what makes them so secure and influential. *Since they can't be bought, they get buy-in from others.* Only their cause can hold them hostage. They're not swayed by money, bribes, blackmail, or public opinion. Incidentally, this trait also makes for effective parents: they love their children but don't worry about being liked by their teenager each week. In doing so, they win their child's respect and love as they age.

This kind of leader is passionate because the stakes are high. Deep down, most people want to participate in something that is *very important* and *almost impossible.* Harriet Tubman had this reality on her side. She would only lead a cause or organization she would be willing to stake everything on. This kind of leader isn't satisfied making widgets; they invest their time in something that pays great dividends. They're forceful not because they have a mean spirit, but because they embody such a high standard and work for such high stakes. Others yearn to experience it, too. Do you remember Steve Jobs's pitch to John Sculley at PepsiCo when asking him to join Apple? He said, "Do you want to sell sugar water for the rest of your life or come with me and change the world?" Sculley said the question hit him like a punch to the gut.

This kind of leader is not an "electoral leader" but often a "radical leader." Alexander the Great once said, "I am not afraid of an army of lions led by a sheep. I am afraid of an army of sheep led by a lion." He meant that everything rises and falls on leadership. An "electoral leader" works best in a constitutional environment, where leaders are seen as representatives of the people, positioned to fulfill their wishes, having been voted into office by the people. Usually they're politicians. "Radical leaders" are like Harriet Tubman. There likely is no vote. This leader steps up to take a courageous role and people vote with their feet, either choosing to join them or continue as they are. Radical leaders raise the bar wherever they go.

This kind of leader realizes that, to retain followers, forgiveness is necessary. The paradox of this uncommon leader is their propensity to forgive people. It's not that they lower their standards. It's simply that they're able to absolve a team member who acknowledges they failed to meet the standard and chooses to improve. Forgiveness isn't approving what happened. It's choosing to rise above it. Forgiveness does not remove the past, but it does expand the future. Because this uncommon leader is focused on a better future, they make a habit of getting beyond past failures by learning from them. These leaders know the most valuable team members will likely make mistakes en route to success. They know it's the cost of doing business.

Let's double-click on this one.

For Harriet Tubman, the forgiveness was more personal.

She once tried to stop the beating of a fellow slave and was hit by a two-pound weight on the head by the slave owner. It knocked her down, broke her skull, leaving a dent from that point on. It also left her lingering near death for weeks. Her decision to intervene came from an inward conviction about human value. Her standard compelled her to act when it was violated. She shared with her biographer, Sarah Bradford, that following the incident, she prayed for her perpetrator's conversion to loving ways long afterward. Can you see both her high standard and her gracious forgiveness toward others who fail to meet it?

While traveling the Underground Railroad, Harriet pulled a gun on those she was leading more than once while en route to the North. This was typically in response to her fellow travelers' fears or doubts about the journey. Yet, more than once, she forgave these folks when they came clean about their weakness. Harriet knew that someone's weak heart or faltering will could put others in danger. She had to bring them to resolve. Yet when they "came to their senses," Harriet was quick to forgive them of their weak moment and release them to continue.

Where have you witnessed this type of uncommon leadership?

Once, Tubman even once found herself face-to-face with one of her "hunters," a slave owner who was part of a posse commissioned to search for her. She had a bounty on her head and several Confederates were determined to capture or kill her. In this instance, Harriet had shot the gun out of his hand and found herself staring at an unarmed enemy. She could have finished him off. She was furious, and he was obstinate, even arrogant, claiming if she shot him, there would be more coming after her. On this occasion she chose to let him go. To this day, we're not sure why.

Such are the qualities of these uncommon leaders. High standards. Gracious forgiveness.

THE PARADOX EXPLAINED

I believe I've met such leaders today. They are rare and extraordinary. These uncommon leaders are sticklers for excellence, demanding more than team members feel they can even offer. In this sense, *they're almost inhuman.* Their high standards separate their organization from others who can only emulate their great products or services. They have over-the-top benchmarks that put them in a league of their own—like Apple, Amazon, Zappos, and Google. At the same time, these leaders balance their standards with a grace to forgive errors made by team members; to offer mercy to those who fall short, empowering them to recover and later rise to the occasion. *This makes them human.*

This combination is precisely what makes them unusual. Our world today places all leaders under a microscope. Everything is scrutinized, filmed, and posted on social media, with viewers constantly leaving "likes" or "dislikes," comments and judgments. In this way, most of us feel like we are being voted upon continually. We are all aware of how quickly opinions travel and how one bad move can equal a trial by the jury of "public opinion." Many a CEO, college president, or athletic coach have lost their jobs after one seemingly innocuous decision that wasn't aligned with public opinion. Too often, a leader's response is to become a sort of politician. It dilutes genuine leadership.

Some goals can never be reached by this kind of leader. What's needed is a "Harriet Tubman" type of leader. One's who cares little about majority opinion and usually proves to be right in the end. This paradoxical leader is different and looks for followers who not only stand in defiance of popular opinion, but who commit to more.

It's why I say their followers do more than merely vote for them. They're all in.

Henry David Thoreau put it this way: "All voting is a sort of gaming, like checkers or backgammon, with a slight moral tinge to it, a playing with right and wrong, with moral questions. . . . The character of the voters is not staked. I cast my vote, perchance as I think right; but I am not vitally concerned that that right should prevail. I am willing to leave it to the majority. Its obligation, therefore, never exceeds that of expediency. Even voting for the right is doing nothing for it. It is only expressing to men feebly your desire that it should prevail."[2]

Uncommon leaders are usually ahead of their time and push others to catch up. When Steve Jobs was asked why he wasn't asking the public what they wanted in his Apple products, he replied, "Some people say, 'Give the customers what they want.' But that's not my approach. Our job is to figure out what they're going to want before they do."

At a 1982 planning retreat, someone on the Mac team "thought they should do some market research to see what customers wanted. 'No,' Jobs replied. 'Because customers don't know what they want until we've shown them.'"

"On the day he unveiled the Macintosh, a reporter from *Popular Science* asked Jobs what type of market research he had done. Jobs responded by scoffing, 'Did Alexander Graham Bell do any market research before he invented the phone?'"

Our world does still need electoral leaders who represent the majority. Yet, it also needs these extraordinary leaders who push for change and require teams that do more than hold their finger in the air to feel which way the wind is blowing. I think Henry Ford once said, "If I'd asked customers what they wanted, they would have told me, 'A faster horse!' People don't know what they want until you show it to them. That's why I never rely on market research. Our task is to read things that are not yet on the page."[3]

How does this look in businesses and organizations?

THIS PARADOX IN REAL LIFE

Serving with John Maxwell between 1983 and 2006, I recognized him as one of these uncommon leaders who possessed high standards yet was very forgiving of those who tried and failed. I was one of those team members. I started with Dr. Maxwell almost right out of college, at twenty-three years old. I didn't want to displease my extraordinary leader, but since I began so young, my journey included a lot of trial and error. I yearned to gain credibility with him and with my colleagues, but I lacked experience. I recall John consistently affirmed my successes, and when I failed, we'd sit down and he'd say, "I'd rather you try and fail than not try at all. Let's figure out what we learned here." John would tell our team, "A person must be big enough to admit his mistakes, smart enough to profit from them, and strong enough to correct them." Over and over, when John saw me pushing myself to improve, he found it within himself to forgive my shortcomings. What he had little patience for was:

- Failing at doing something "average" rather than something great.
- Doing what was expected and assuming we'd receive accolades.
- Failing to try at all in the name of playing it safe. He hated "survival mode."

Herein lies the psychology of this paradox.

When team members know their leader holds high standards, yet is willing to forgive mistakes, it frees them to push themselves, take appropriate risks, and initiate when they might normally hold back and play it safe. Regulations cause people to perform out of duty. Leaders with high expectations and a capacity to forgive mistakes motivate people to perform out of devotion. These are the two most common factors that motivate team members: duty or devotion. Leaders choose the motivation of their followers through their leadership style. Forgiveness is the emotional connection that allows a leader to hold high standards, gain effort, and not lose their followers. This is true for parents and their children. It's true for coaches and their athletes. It's also true for managers and their teams.

Here's why these two characteristics must be combined.

If you don't possess high standards, and you offer gracious forgiveness, your people will not be incentivized to perform at their best. Average expectations with an "easy out" lead to mediocrity. People will put work on "cruise control" or "autopilot" and likely do the bare minimum that's expected.

If you possess high standards and don't offer forgiveness, your people will be incentivized to only do the safe thing. They won't take risks. They won't attempt anything that isn't a sure thing. They'll stay in bounds so as not to put their jobs at risk.

Either way, people don't exceed expectations. They require someone else to set the bar much of the time. Sadly, most people rely on policies and legislation to tell them what to do and how to think. Without an outsider challenging them to a higher level, they seek and find comfort zones. Uncommon leaders embrace the words of Don Thurman who said, "If you limit yourself to what is comfortable, you'll deny yourself what is possible." So, they push for more.

Let's double-click on this to see why this uncommon leadership is so essential.

THE SINISTER PULL TOWARD AVERAGE

Last year, a minor league baseball manager said to me, "I can't figure out our young ballplayers today. They hit .211 in single A ball, and think it's good enough to be called up to double A." Then, he smiled as if an epiphany had just struck him. He looked at me and said, "Maybe that's the problem. All they're targeting is 'good enough.'"

Our society today unwittingly encourages our kids to simply "blend in." To do what's asked of them, but only what's asked. We condition them to attain the bare minimum requirement, to look for loopholes and shortcuts. They're conditioned to study a topic only if it's going to be on the test or to do a good deed only if they can post it on social media. We don't ask them to venture outside the norm. Average is OK. And anything above average feels quite satisfying.

Wait a moment, you might be thinking. *Aren't more students making As in school than ever before?* The answer is yes, but that fact loses its potency when you consider what's happened. We changed our definition of excellent. Students' grades have been on the rise for over forty years, not so much because they are smarter than children decades ago, but because grades have been inflated by schools. In the 1960s, the average grade given was a C. Why? Because C means average. Today, the average grade is an A.[4] Many adults fear students cannot handle the harsh reality of a C. I spoke in one school district where faculty told me they were not allowed to use red ink when grading papers; it was too harsh. Some teachers told me they were not permitted to use the word "no" because it was too negative.

Culture's message is: "Just finish the work and we'll tell you you're awesome." Too many gifted young athletes, academicians, and other performers embody this "good enough" mindset. They are fine with being "average." Walt Whitman saw a "great average bulk" emerging and wrote:

> Our leading men are not of much account and never have been, but the average of the people is immense, beyond all history. Sometimes I think in all departments, literature and art included, that will be the way our superiority will exhibit itself. We will not have great individuals

or great leaders, but a great average bulk, unprecedentedly great.

THE PROBLEM WITH LETTING OTHERS SET THE STANDARD

What's wrong with being average? Why must we push ourselves for more? You tell me.

- The average American today is 23 pounds overweight.
- The average American spends 103 percent of their income.
- The average American is $90,460 in debt.
- The average American tells 4 lies a day, or 1,460 a year.
- The average American spends 27.5 hours a week on entertainment.
- The average student takes 6 years to finish college, changing majors 4 times.

Growing satisfied with being average or even above average doesn't seem bad, but consider how sinister it can be when we let others set the standard for our satisfaction.

1. Being average is a moving target in society that can easily be diluted.
2. An average goal rarely pushes us to use our talent to its fullest.
3. Average makes us compare ourselves to others . . . and we're unique.
4. Average doesn't encourage us to excel. We are okay with fitting into the "mean score."

Being average means you're as close to the bottom as you are to the top. You are the worst of the best and the best of the worst. Is that really you? Don't you possess some ability or some ambition beyond average? Of course you do. It's time to leverage it. People need leaders to call out the uncommon strengths that lie inside them. Without this push, most succumb to a gravitational pull toward average.

MOVING FROM AVERAGE TO UNCOMMON

The following ideas aren't new or impossible. They are simply rare among people. How many of these principles are you practicing?

1. **Let "average" be your starting point.** It represents the middle of achievement. While we shouldn't settle for average, it's good to see what others have done. Each generation stands on the shoulders of those who've gone before. Runner Roger Bannister (see page 189) began with the then-current mile time and worked from there.
2. **Identify your strengths to find areas you're naturally above average.** Our greatest growth and best chance to stand out lie in the areas of our natural strengths. Michael Jordan said, "All I knew was I didn't want to be average. I didn't come here to be average." We must know and leverage our unique traits.
3. **Research enough to embrace an ideal and set a new standard.** "Great minds discuss ideas. Average minds discuss events. Small minds discuss people," said Eleanor Roosevelt. I believe she's right. We cannot be satisfied with repeating what's already been done. Look for new horizons and ask: Why

not? If you want the next time to be better than the last time, you must do something different in the meantime.

4. **Determine a need and opportunity that matches your identity.** It has been said, "Don't seek your passion. Chase opportunity and you'll naturally find it." Being exceptional can only be achieved by those who devote themselves to needs and causes that are bigger than themselves. We achieve greatness by our relation to important causes, movements, and achievements.
5. **Each day, work to improve 1 percent above what you've done.** Find one step you can take each day that pushes you beyond average. "How do you win?" asked Bum Phillips. "By getting average players to play good and good players to play great. That's how you win." Excellence occurs one step at a time.
6. **Give it all you've got until you've excelled and it's measurable.** The dream is free. The hustle is sold separately. The one element that separates dreamers from doers is effort. Anyone who's ever taken a shower has gotten a good idea. The key is to dry off after the shower and go after it.
7. **Find and associate with people who share your ambitions.** Jim Rohn said it best: "You are the average of the five people you spend the most time with." Those who excel above average spend time around other excellent people. Henry Ford, Thomas Edison, and Harvey Firestone took fishing trips together. All three changed the way we lived our lives.

Where do you see symptoms of a "good enough" attitude in our culture?

8. **Avoid the soft bigotry of low expectations.** Run from those who let you remain lazy and unchallenged. While we need days of rest, our best "self" surfaces in times of rigor. I am at my best laboring somewhere between *stretched* and *overwhelmed.* Like rubber bands, we're only useful when we're stretched.

The most intriguing truth to me is this—excelling is within the reach of everyone. Being "above average" is not necessarily difficult, just rare. Question: How long does it take the average person to earn a black belt? Answer: The average person does not earn a black belt. It is a person, large or small, gifted or ungifted, who refuses to settle for average. This means excellence may look different to different people. Yet, it's reachable for everyone. If you really want something, you'll find a way. If you don't, you'll find an excuse.

Who do you know who excels, but not necessarily because they're gifted? What qualities do you see in them that enable them to be excellent?

One of our *Habitudes*® is called "the Encore Effect." Great leaders and effective communicators practice it. They offer something beyond what people expected. At a concert, a band steps back onto the stage after their last song on the setlist and performs one more show-stopping tune that brings the audience to their feet. It's an encore.

I think uncommon leaders do this for people as well.

They follow through on what teammates require of them, but then they also choose to go the extra mile. They serve a bit more. Smile a bit more. They add a bit more value. They're prone to say: "I woke up this morning and realized I don't have what it takes to sit back and be average."

THE UNEXPECTED CHARACTERISTIC THAT EMPOWERS PEOPLE TO MEET A STANDARD

Unfortunately, pushing people to be and do more is a complicated issue. If it were only about persuading them to excel, every organization in the world would meet all its standards. But they don't. The average person can see your "high standard" but frequently can't hit it because of their insecurities, not their lack of talent or desire. There are emotional deficits inside of the average person that prevent them from pushing themselves to meet a standard.

This why leaders must understand another *Habitude®*, the "Golden Gate Paradox."

The building of the Golden Gate Bridge was a stunning feat in engineering. Bridge construction began in 1933, in the midst of the Great Depression. The unemployment rate was 25 percent, so people were looking for jobs. With the exception of some very specialized tasks, the bridge was built by a local labor force. Workers were proud to be part of one of the most incredible achievements of the industrial revolution.

What you may not know is, the Golden Gate Bridge is also a story of astonishing achievements in safety standards. The expectation at the time for steel bridge construction was one fatality for every $1 million in cost. By those standards, the safety record for the Golden Gate Bridge was impressive: only eleven workers died completing the $35 million project. How did they pull this off?

Typically, when someone fell and died during a bridge's construction, work slowed down. Remaining workers became apprehensive and fearful. Deadlines were missed as men became preoccupied with *survival* rather than *success* on the project. Foremen became pushy as workers became cautious. After all, time is money.

Chief engineer Joseph Strauss was convinced, however, that although deadlines might be missed, workers needed to labor safely. So, Strauss made the site the first in America to have a safety net suspended underneath them. The decision was a costly one at $130,000, but it worked. The net saved the lives of nineteen falling workers, who called themselves the "Halfway to Hell Club." Not only did people survive, but the work sped up as everyone felt empowered to focus on completing their work rather than on their own safety. Despite the cost of the pricey safety net, the project was finished on time, on budget, and with minimal casualties.

Can you see the paradox?

Suspending a safety net underneath a project costs both money and time. A leader might assume it's not worth the cost. Ironically, however, it saves time and cash. The work accelerates as teams feel safe, empowered, and able to focus on getting the job done. They don't fear for their lives.

This is a decision all life-giving leaders make.

Uncommon leaders create an environment where team members aren't afraid to fall, to falter, or to fail. It's as though they place an imaginary "safety net" under the team. Suddenly, success comes more quickly because failure isn't final or fatal. The net enables team members to succeed and to succeed quickly. They're concerned with doing their job well instead of keeping their job.

Do you recall the infamous story of Tom Watson Jr., the CEO of IBM between 1956 and 1971? Tom was a central figure in the information revolution. One of his young executives made some poor decisions that cost the company several million dollars. He was summoned to Watson's office, fully expecting to be dismissed from his job. As he entered the office, he decided to speak first. "I suppose after that set of mistakes, you will want to fire me," the young man said. Watson surprised him by replying: "Not at all, young man. We have just spent a couple of million dollars educating you."[5]

WHY THIS LEADERSHIP PARADOX WORKS

For several years now, our focus groups have informed us that team members today have an extreme fear of failure. I believe in part that this is the fault of culture's message to everyone: *Whatever you do, don't make a mistake. Don't get it wrong. Don't fail.* Folks often feel lots of anxiety, and the pressure to perform perfectly on every level.

A 2012 study posted in the *Journal of Experimental Psychology* discovered this pressure can have a negative effect on learning. In several experiments, researchers found that respondents will perform self-protective acts, and avoid any potentially risky challenge where failure is an option.[6] Another study found that anxiety disengages the prefrontal cortex, a region of the brain that plays an important role in flexible decision-making.[7] We have trouble making good choices when we are anxious about the results. According to new studies published in the *Journal of Educational Psychology*, "these students set the bar low, setting safe goals they're confident can be achieved. They're chronic underachievers."[8] I hope this isn't your team.

Most leaders I know believe they have, indeed, created an environment where it's okay to make mistakes. Their team members, however, might say otherwise. What would those you lead say about you? My interviews reveal that too many are absolutely terrified they might do something wrong. They hold back, performing at below average levels, or they simply disengage. A 2015 report from Gallup shows 51 percent of the US workforce is "not engaged" at work.

WHAT COULD YOUR TEAM LOOK LIKE?

My guess is, you've heard about organizations that practice the *Golden Gate Paradox* well. Years ago, I first heard that the 3M company not only encouraged risk taking but gave team members 15 percent of their week to experiment on projects they had dreamed up themselves. Chairman William McKnight would walk around spotting employees working on zany ideas and he got excited about them, providing a sense of *anticipation* rather than *anxiety* about them. It paid off. Many of the products we use on a weekly basis were the result of these zany ideas, including Post-it notes, Scotch tape, Scotch transparent tape, Wetordry waterproof sandpaper, and rubber cement. All of these were created because the culture was life-giving and created safe spaces to make mistakes.

As I review what made 3M great, I think it was McKnight's paradoxical rule of management:

- Set a high standard for people to meet. (This stretches them to excel.)
- Model consistent forgiveness when they fail. (This enables them to risk.)

Summary of this paradox

WHEN I SET HIGH STANDARDS	WHEN I OFFER GRACIOUS FORGIVENESS
1. I challenge people to strive for excellence.	1. I enable people to take risks on the way.
2. I enable people to perform better.	2. I encourage people to push harder.
3. No one settles for mediocre outcomes.	3. No one worries about disappointing a leader.
4. People are motivated toward excellence.	4. People are inspired because they're safe.
5. I offer targets to hit.	5. I offer safety nets to fall into.
6. Teams do more than they felt possible.	6. Teams do more than they felt possible.

Steps to take to practice this paradox

To create this kind of environment, try this leadership path:

1. **Offer the Gift of Clarity.** Make sure the people you lead understand what a "win" looks like. At the end of a project, what is the specific outcome you're shooting for? What is the clear objective? Ensure that everyone is on the same page. People must be aligned and energized by the target.
2. **Shoot for perfection and settle for excellence.** This is a phrase we've used on our team for years. We will always shoot for perfection. Plans are to pull off an event or product or service perfectly. Yet we know, human error is a normal cost of doing business. So, we shoot for the sun and may hit the moon. Excellence is OK.
3. **Communicate your high expectations but model your forgiveness.** You cannot practice this paradox in word alone. Your team must see you embody it in more than speeches—they likely won't believe it until they see it modeled. No one wants to be the guinea pig. Find occasions to communicate huge goals and model generous forgiveness.
4. **Do not hide your own accountability to both high standards and self-forgiveness.** I remember making a huge error and feeling horrible about it. It cost our team publicity and brand equity. It diminished our marketing efforts. I knew our team needed a clinic from me in taking responsibility. With them watching, I worked hard to win back what was lost and make a point of forgiving myself for my mistake.
5. **Extend the Safety Net Principle.** Let people know they have equal parts responsibility and autonomy

to get their jobs done. Give them the freedom to try and make mistakes, while "owning" the project they are working on. Ultimately, they're free to fail on their journey toward finding a way to get the job done.

6. **Practice "Try It Out and Talk It Over."** Team members feel safer to make mistakes and even fail if they know they are free to try out something new, record the results, and then meet with a leader to discuss the outcomes. At Growing Leaders, we encourage team members to try things, but we always "talk it over" once a project is complete to talk about how we could improve the next time. As Jim Collins reminds us, "shoot bullets before cannonballs." Try out a small pilot project and see what hits the target before going big.
7. **"Manage by Walking Around."** In this kind of environment, both creativity and mistakes will surface. You must be okay with both. You can minimize damage by practicing what Tom Peters calls MBWA: *Manage by Walking Around.* Daily, stroll around to check out what's going on.
8. **Recruit good people and trust the process.** Once you get the right people in the right places on the team, do your best to trust the process you've created and the people you've hired to run it. While failure will happen, the price is worth it. Your people will learn, good things will be created, and the benefit will ultimately outweigh the costs.
9. **Ask the right questions to learn from mistakes.** Instead of drawing conclusions or offering lectures—try leading with questions. Why did the mistake occur? Do they need more clarity and

direction? Do they need extra support? Be sure the questions communicate that you care and that you're confident in their abilities.

10. **Express belief.** This is the key action on your part. Be sure what you say and do relays belief in them. Discern what would communicate confidence in them, high expectations of them, and hope for them. Strong belief inspires strong behavior.
11. **Follow through.** Finally, whatever belief you've communicated, follow through in demonstrating its credibility. Don't undo what you've said with negativity or contradictory words. Be sure your actions match your words. This will help them "own" their work.

You may have heard of Roy "Wrong Way" Riegels. He was the NCAA football player who became famous when he picked up a fumble, and in his excitement, ran the wrong way, toward the opposing team's end zone in the 1929 Rose Bowl. Roy was tackled by his own teammate just before scoring for the other team. He got up absolutely humiliated. He said later it was the worst day of his life.

What you may not know is that, during halftime, Coach Nibs Price said nothing about it. He gave an energizing pep talk, then said, "All right—I want the same team to start the second half that started the first half."

Riegels couldn't believe it. In his disbelief, he just sat there refusing to return to the field. With great discernment, Coach Price said to him as they sat alone in the locker room, "Roy—I believe in you. If you don't go out there and play this second half, everyone will remember you for what you just did in the first half. You owe it to yourself to show us all who you really are."

Coach Price said later he'd never seen anyone play with more passion and intelligence than Roy Riegels did in that second half.

All Roy "Wrong Way" Riegels needed was an uncommon leader with a safety net.

THINK IT THROUGH, TALK IT OVER

- Do you know leaders who balance these two qualities well?
- What do you struggle with as you lead: high standards or gracious forgiveness?
- Why do you suppose radical leaders are so rare? Do you consider yourself one?
- What must you do to improve practicing this paradox?

PARADOX 8

Uncommon Leaders Are Both Timely and Timeless

Warren Susman wrote that political historians will call the 1930s the age of Franklin Roosevelt. But cultural historians will likely call the 1930s the age of Walt Disney.[1] During that decade of economic depression, Disney found ways to entertain and encourage the public, touching their hearts with a needed message. His cartoons were filled with zany story lines (reflecting the crazy ups and downs of the US economy), but he always resolved the conflict by returning to timeless traditions. He connected the past to the present and he connected the present to the future. Millions consider him an "entertainment genius."

Part of his genius was that Walt Disney loved the past and the future.

He was a man of sentiment and a man of hope. Consequently, he believed that stories should call listeners to hold on to the timeless virtues of our past, all the while grasping at the future hopes of a better tomorrow in America.

WALT DISNEY WAS THE KING OF IMAGINATION

Walt was ignited by imagination. He was at his best when he was able to use it. His gait was fast, and few could keep up with him. The guardrails for him were only two:

1. Honor and learn from what's in the past.
2. Imagine and strive for a preferred future.

"Uncle Walt," as he was called by many who knew him, became known for conservative and wholesome values in the 1950s. Much has been written about this. Journalists said he was the *personification of traditional values and square aesthetics,* producing shows celebrating patriotism (the Hall of Presidents), family values (the Mickey Mouse Club) and the American frontier (Davy Crockett mania swept the country in 1955). As the world grew more modern (in the 1950s and 60s), Walt stood at the forefront of the imaginative progress, while at the same time calling America back to its roots. You might say he was both *progressive* and *conservative.* He built a model train set in his home. Yet he was also obsessed with science, space travel, computer technology, and robots.

He was an anomaly to be able to straddle both. His leadership was paradoxical.

Walt was enthralled by the future. On November 15, 1965, he met with Florida governor Haydon Burns at a press conference to introduce plans for the future Walt Disney World complex. Truth be told, Walt had less interest in the theme parks and more in the experimental city connected to it. EPCOT is an acronym standing for the Experimental Prototype Community of Tomorrow. It was designed to be a utopian city of the future that Walt Disney envisioned would combine "city" and "community" in one place. The EPCOT Center eventually became known as, simply, Epcot, and illustrates what captured Walt's imagination the final years of his life. "Epcot was originally conceived by Disney during the early development of Walt Disney World, as an experimental planned community that would serve as a center for American innovation and urban living."[2] At its entrance is Spaceship Earth, where the history and future of communication is represented. As a cultural and entertainment leader, Walt spoke to your mind and your heart. As you walk through his original theme park, you see his focus on being timely and timeless.

Disneyland includes throwbacks to American towns centuries ago:

- Adventureland
- Frontierland
- Main Street USA

At the same time, the park ignites our imagination of what life could look like in the future:

- Tomorrowland
- Fantasyland
- Star Wars: Galaxy's Edge

You feel nostalgic and enticed. Your imagination is triggered by both. Walt attempted to pass on his love for *progress* as well as *tradition* to everyone. One of the early brochures for the theme park read: *When you enter Disneyland, you'll find yourself in the land of yesterday and tomorrow and fantasy. Nothing of the present exists in Disneyland.*[3] Walt believed the present is informed by the past and the future. For decades, the park included "The Carousel of Progress," a production showcasing how American life evolved over the last one hundred years, then predicting where it might go in the future. Walt was careful to show the upgrades and updates of a typical American home yet at the same time remind us of how we retain the same needs for relationships, love, and communication.

Uncommon leaders balance these realities.

UNCOMMON LEADERS ARE TIMELY AND TIMELESS

Uncommon leaders in the twenty-first century must balance this very difficult paradox. First, they must embrace and advance timeless principles that make for lasting success; values that have stood the test of time and worked in all generations and in every context. At the same time, these leaders must leverage culturally relevant methods and futuristic resources. They use what is cultural to say what is evergreen. Their core identity is ageless, but their mode of operation is cutting edge and sets the pace for others. They're passionate to pursue future opportunity, but in their appetite for progress, they never leave behind core virtues, values, and disciplines.

- To thirst for progress alone is incomplete.
- To cling to past values alone in incomplete.
- Excellence requires teams to embrace both.

Excellence was one of Disney's timeless values. It defined all his ventures from the start. During the 1940s, Walt took his daughters to ride a merry-go-round at a local park. He saw how pitiful it looked and operated. Several of the horses were scuffed and needed to be repainted. With each ride, he watched his girls trying to find a horse that went up and down as it should. While sitting on a bench watching them, he wrote himself a note about the park he would build one day: "No chipped paint; all horses go up and down."

Mr. Disney was ruthless in cutting anything in a film that obstructed the story's pacing and plot. It had to be excellent. Ward Kimball, one of the animators of Disney's *Snow White and the Seven Dwarfs,* recalls working 240 days on a four-and-a-half-minute sequence in which the dwarfs made soup for Snow White and almost destroyed the kitchen in the process. Disney thought it was funny, but he decided the scene stopped the flow of the picture.

Although there had been lots of talent and energy invested, plus two-thirds of a year spent on that scene, Walt cut it.

Walt's insistence on excellence and his fondness for the past made Americans feel safe enough to join him in his exploration of the unknown future. *He was one of them, but he was in front of them.*

This is how Walt married the past to the future.

He kept his eye on both *trends* and *traditions.* He embraced the new to remind us of the old. One vivid illustration of this was his move from a partnership with ABC to NBC studios in 1960. At this point in television history, TVs were making their move from black and white programs to color. NBC took his program called *Walt Disney Presents* and renamed it *Walt Disney's Wonderful World of Color.* They turned him loose to create twenty-five programs in color using his imagination about yesterday and tomorrow. What was their incentive? Walt represented where America was going and RCA, NBC's parent company, had just invested lots of money manufacturing color TVs. With Walt in charge of a show that had "color" in its title, they felt sure it would help sell televisions. And they were right. Shortly after the premier of *Walt Disney's Wonderful World of Color,* Card Walker, who led advertising at NBC studios, wrote Walt to tell him that sales of color televisions were soaring—105 percent ahead of the previous September.[4]

Biographer Neal Gabler summarized Disney by saying, "He was king . . . of American pop culture. With the success of Disneyland and his visibility on the television show, Walt Disney's personal status was higher than it had ever been—as high as anyone's in the country. The Screen Producers Guild unanimously voted him its Lewis Milestone Award for his 'historical contribution to the American motion picture.' The United States Olympic Committee appointed him chairman of its Pageantry Committee for the 1960 Winter Games . . . and Walt planned and oversaw the torch relay, the opening and closing ceremonies and the awarding of the medals. President Eisenhower named him to the President's Committee on Education and President Kennedy appointed Walt to a nine-member executive committee to lead the People to People program, which was designed to promote cultural, scientific and athletic contacts between countries."[5] Walt Disney has schools named after him and colleges that awarded him honorary doctorates, even though his formal education never went beyond ninth grade.

Let's examine the transferrable concepts that made this leader uncommon.

LOOKING FOR THE OLD AND THE NEW

In 2017, I wrote a book called *Marching Off the Map* with my colleague Andrew McPeak. It's built on the premise that we must lead our teams into new territory, not merely master the property we currently possess. I tell the story of Alexander the Great, who wasn't satisfied with conquering the known world but marched his three armies into territories for which we had no maps yet. He transformed some of his soldiers into "mapmakers"—requiring them to draw new maps as they discovered new lands, sketching out the rivers, hills, plains, mountains, and valleys.

Can you imagine? They literally had to draw the maps as they marched.

This had to be both exhilarating and frightening. They mapped as they marched. They penned as they progressed. They were training as they were traveling. It would have been useless to continue using old maps in this new territory.

This is where we live today, and it still isn't easy.

It never has been. Even in ancient days, people loved the familiar even with so much yet to explore. Folks didn't embrace new "mapmakers" like Copernicus, or Newton, or Galileo. Even Christopher Columbus couldn't get funding from his own country for his trip. They assumed the world was flat. Yet, since his day, new maps have expanded rapidly. Especially since the enlightenment, change has been happening on a growth curve that makes most people shudder. Discoveries are made, and yet they are questioned and shunned. We can't seem to "see" what's coming. Case in point. In 2006, CNN listed Mark Zuckerberg on the list of "10 People Who Don't Matter." In 2004, Bill Gates said: "Two years from now, spam will be solved." And in 1997, Nathan Myhrvold, former Microsoft CTO, said: "Apple is already dead." Twenty years earlier, Ken Olsen, the founder of Digital Equipment Corporation, said, "There's no reason anyone would want a computer in their home."

The unknown produces fear in us. This is especially true today as we live on the other side of the COVID-19 pandemic. Even with greater scientific knowledge and better technology than ever, life remains uncertain. Do you remember seeing a picture of a map drawn centuries ago? In one corner of those maps, where the ocean lay, the mapmaker would always draw a dragon or sea serpent, as if to say: *Out here, we don't know what exists. Be afraid; be very afraid.*

Yet, Alexander continued marching. His armies created maps we've benefited from today.

We must not forget, however, as Alexander the Great progressed through new territory, he and his soldiers looked for the familiar—they needed water to drink, food to eat, and they observed the same sun to recognize the time of day and season of the year. In other words, as they made new discoveries, they also embraced timeless resources they would always need. It was a constant combination. Leaders must find ways to progress into new territory without neglecting the water and food. We must embrace the *new* but retain the *necessary*.

I love how Lin-Manuel Miranda blended the timeless and timely to both teach and entertain. Miranda wrote the music, lyrics, and script for the musical production *Hamilton*, which opened on Broadway in 2015. In its first year, it was nominated for an unprecedented sixteen Tony Awards and won eleven of them. I believe Miranda's genius lies in his combination of a timeless rags-to-riches story with the timely genre of rap music. It's stunning. Yesterday's story; today's style. Timeless and timely.

Let's try an exercise to help us practice this paradox.

SWING SETS AND PLUMB LINES

Two metaphors have been useful to me as I attempt to practice this paradox: a swing set and a plumb line. Let's examine these and allow them to guide us into good decisions.

I want you to think about a swing set. Did you or a neighbor have one growing up? We installed one in our Atlanta home, while our children were young. It provided hours of amusement for all of us, as we swung our kids back and forth.

Back and forth.

I believe a swing set is a helpful image of what we must do to lead well in our day. Just like a good swing, you must swing backward as far as possible, to swing forward as high as possible. Do you remember your children giggling as they yelled, "Higher! Swing me higher, Mommy!"

> Which do you embrace most naturally: the timely or the timeless?

Wise leaders utilize vision that can see both *backward* and *forward.* They look back and learn from the past. They glean from past mistakes to avoid repeating them. They seek what was helpful and timeless so they can carry those elements forward. They do this so they can swing forward well. That's the engaging part of the ride, the swing forward. Far too often, leaders grab only one of these two elements. They're only looking backward, feverishly attempting to grip the past, fearing they might lose everything they hold dear. Or they only swing forward, lusting for progress so much, they care little about how it may affect people morally or socially.

- One is primarily about caution and conserving.
- One is primarily about progress and profit.

Once again, neither is complete without the other.

HOW DO YOU APPLY THIS?

To implement this kind of leadership, you must push "pause" and reflect on both the past and the future. I recommend you take time each year, if not each quarter, and use this exercise to stay on top of life and leadership. Grab a pen and respond to the following questions.

Swinging backward

Swinging back means we get in touch with our heritage—our roots. Who we are, and how we got here today. We identify our foundation, both positive and negative. As we do, it is helpful to ask ourselves questions like:

- What is our foundation and heritage?
- Why did we decide to pursue our mission?
- What value did we seek to add to our community?
- What were the destructive elements we tried to discard?
- Were there principles we felt are essential to sustain us?

Swinging forward

Swinging forward means we haven't forgotten why we exist and won't lose our sense of mission as we progress. We identify our new realities and translate our mission for today's culture. Helpful questions might be:

- Where do we want to go today?
- What are the greatest needs we see in front of us?
- How is the landscape different than it was in the past?
- What new methods or strategies do we need in the future?
- How do we stay relevant by renewing our pledge to our mission?

PLUMB LINES

My second metaphor, beyond the swing set, is a plumb line. It's another picture of what we need today. Do you remember what a plumb line is?

It's a long string that has a weight attached to the end of it. A plumb line was used in the past to measure *depth* and *accuracy*. Most often it was a cord weighted with lead that was used to plumb the depths of an ocean or lake. A fisherman could drop the weight in the water and use it to determine how deep it was. But plumb lines also measure accuracy. For centuries, they were held next to a wall in a building to evaluate if vertical structures were true. While next to a wall, gravity pulled the cord straight down, making it easy to see if a wall was crooked. These two purposes made plumb lines essential for centuries:

- The depth of the water.
- The direction of the wall.

Through the years, these plumb lines were used as symbols in literature. They represented a standard by which one could evaluate whether something was off and did not meet a standard.

In 2020, my wife and I moved out of our house to have it renovated. Builders came in to reconstruct our kitchen, expand our windows, put new floors down, and move a wall. I had the opportunity to visit each week and check on their progress. I also took advantage of my chance to hold a plumb line up to a load-bearing post to observe if it was crooked or straight. I knew the builders had used a level on it, but I wanted to see for myself that it was perfectly perpendicular. You don't want a load-bearing wall to have the slightest angle or it could collapse.

How can you utilize the past to leverage the future?

So it is with leaders and teams.

The fact is, when we build anything new, we must hold a "plumb line" next to it to ensure it matches our values. We need plumb lines in every industry, school, athletic team, and home to help us measure how deep we are or if we've gotten crooked. Metaphorically speaking, they are timeless *standards* that we agree to be a healthy measuring stick for *character* and *conduct.* Historically, our US judicial system has used the Bill of Rights as a "plumb line" to check precedents and to examine if an activity has become "crooked." We even used to call criminals "crooks." My question is—do you have plumb lines for your work?

What does this look like, as we lead today? What are your plumb lines for your team?

- What are your plumb lines for excellence?
- What are your plumb lines for innovation?
- What are your plumb lines for ethics and values?
- What are your plumb lines for the pace of change?
- What are your plumb lines for trust on the team?
- What are your plumb lines for inclusion and diversity?
- What are your plumb lines for adding value to the community?

Author C. S. Lewis summarized it best: "We all want progress, but if you're on the wrong road progress means doing an about turn and walking back to the right road. In that case, the man who turns back the soonest is the one who is most progressive."

WHY IS THIS SO CRUCIAL TODAY?

Leaders are at greater risk of losing either the ability to be "timely" and "timeless" than in past eras. Why? First, because everyone is in a race toward new innovations to stay ahead of the pack. Second, because smart technology enables us to change rapidly. Sadly, COVID-19 forced too many of us into a survival mode in which we ignore either the timely or timeless. Today, many leaders and organizations will fail to morph fast enough to the new realities thrust upon us by the pandemic. Businesses, schools, shopping, travel, healthcare, and events will likely never be the same. During the initial quarantine, many companies were unready for the changes it required and shut down. Others, however, grew stronger than ever, including Amazon, Zoom, Clorox, Slack, Nintendo, 3M, and many more. Why? They were poised for this new digital age.

By the same token, many will fail to remain timeless because of our appetite for progress, and the need for speed to market. This is exacerbated by the fact that we live in a world where our portable devices are smart; our cars are smart, our homes are smart, and our online commerce is smart. I wonder—will we, as leaders, maintain our ethics? Will our morals erode because expansion is more important? Let's be honest—artificial intelligence enables us to go places we may not be ready for morally. Kevin Kelly said it best: "Our smart technology advances so quickly, it outpaces our ability to civilize it."[6]

LEADING IN A TIMELY WAY THROUGH THE AGES

In every era, leaders must recognize the critical component is to thrive. This key component shifts over time, so it is a moving target. Michael Bloomberg gave a university commencement speech years ago that inspired me to think through this idea. I built upon his initial thought and offer below a summary of how industry has changed over time and what the great need of the hour is today. You can see below I've outlined the four major eras humanity has experienced, in the left-hand column below. On the right, I summarized the critical component to thrive in each era. Now that we live in the "age of intelligence" with smart devices everywhere, the need for timeless morals and ethics, in my opinion, surges to the top of the list as critical.

HISTORICAL AGE	CRITICAL ELEMENT TO THRIVE
1. Agricultural Age	1. Our muscles
2. Industrial Age	2. Our machines
3. Information Age	3. Our minds
4. Intelligence Age	4. Our morals

Millennia ago, we needed good muscles to get ahead. Centuries ago, we began to need good machines to get ahead. Decades ago, as we entered the information age, most of us made our money with our minds, not our muscles. Today, however, our computers are intelligent, often smarter than we are. In such times, we'd best possess a moral compass.

When we possess plumb lines, we're free to change rapidly, because we know who we are. Even a fast rate of change is less frightening because our identity and ethics are intact. We can morph with accelerated speed to market because we're not "zigzagging" but adapting to new realities. Angela Ahrendt's parting words to the 2012 Leadercast audience were: "Don't get intimidated by the speed of the world. However, the faster we move, the more important it is to remember our values." We must recognize that *exciting* doesn't always equal *better*, *expanding* does not always equal *progress*. A flood is water expanding, but it usually causes damage. Alfred Montapert said, "Do not confuse motion with progress. A rocking horse keeps moving but does not make any progress." Growth always means change, but change does not always equate to growth.

Our movement must lead to improvement.

It's all about leaders promoting:

Timeless principles.

Timely progress.

WHAT DOES "TIMELY" LOOK LIKE?

In 1945, Noah McVicker worked at Kutol Products, a Cincinnati-based soap manufacturer. The Kroger grocery store chain asked Kutol to create a product that could clean coal residue from wallpaper. Back then, homes were coal heated but as it burned it left a dark stain on the walls. McVicker created a putty-like substance that was sticky and could take the soot off any wall.

Following World War II, however, homes transitioned from coal heating to natural gas, and the need for this product decreased substantially. Not only that, but vinyl-based wallpaper had been invented, which also reduced the need for a cleaning product for walls. The Kutol company began to decline, and within a few years, was near bankruptcy.

Noah McVicker's nephew, Joe, joined Kutol to save the company. Joe McVicker's sister-in-law, Kay, was a nursery-school teacher who'd seen a newspaper ad about making art projects with wallpaper cleaning products. It was a creative way to repurpose the irrelevant product. She persuaded Noah and Joe to manufacture their putty as a child's toy. When she tried it with her students, they loved it. Kay and her husband suggested the name: Play-Doh.

Joe took Play-Doh to an educational convention for manufacturers of school supplies. A department store named Woodward and Lothrop decided to sell the compound. In 1956, the McVickers formed the Rainbow Crafts Company to make and sell Play-Doh. Later that year, Macy's and Marshall Field's opened retail accounts and the company was off and running. Over time, Rainbow Crafts merged with other companies like General Mills, Kenner, and Tonka. It was eventually bought by Hasbro in 1991. Along the way, new ways of selling the product surfaced like the Play-Doh Fun Factory and the Creativity Table. Play-Doh is still flourishing to this day.

What can we learn about staying timely from this story?

1. This leader began by listening to customers talk about what they needed.
2. When needs changed, he didn't cling to old methods or insist on irrelevant goals.
3. He stayed open and listened to ideas about how to repurpose his product.
4. He made the changes necessary to become relevant to a whole new audience.
5. He created a product his customers would love before they knew they'd want it.
6. He was willing to learn a new industry and adapt his product to be relevant.

7. He eventually formed partnerships and took his product around the world.

Max McKeown said, "All failure is a failure to adapt. All success is successful adaptation." H&R Block illustrates being timely. Unlike Kutol, however, they switched up their product but kept the same goal. Their mission was to assist Americans with their finances. They began as a bookkeeping company for small businesses that didn't have the revenue to pay a full-time bookkeeper. To draw customers, they offered a tax service for free. When the IRS stopped offering a free tax preparation service to citizens, the need for bookkeepers remained stagnant while the demand from customers for a tax service tripled. Henry and Richard Bloch began focusing on tax services and tripled their revenue in a year. Today, we know H&R Block as a tax company, not for bookkeeping. Same mission. Different offering.

Repurposing our work will be an essential skill to remain timely.

FINDING DRAFTERS TO HELP YOU ADAPT

To remain timely, uncommon leaders identify other leaders who enable them to adapt well. They find others who are ahead of the pack in their industry and glean from them. Even when we are successful, we need others to ensure our success doesn't blind us to the next big adaptation that will be necessary.

Here is a common scenario.

Growing companies can be victims of their own success. They grow, surpass goals, and set records. They get bigger and grow proud of their work. Next, they become satisfied. They're better than they've ever been. But now the key producers are needed as managers, and they don't have time to sell as much. They're managing a team that may or may not share the same entrepreneurial spirit they founded with. This is why the second and third tier of team members can lack the passion or focus of the first out of the gate. This is why we need drafters.

Roger Bannister's story has been told countless times. He did what the world assumed was impossible in 1954. He ran a mile in under four minutes. But it was a team effort. He accomplished the feat with the help of "drafting." Two young men, about as fast as he was, Chris Chataway and Chris Brasher, each ran in front of him, enabling him to run in their draft. The first Chris paced him for the first half mile, then dropped back, when the second Chris sped up and ran ahead of Roger to pace him for the second half. By creating a draft and keeping him up to speed, quite literally, Roger finished in a record 3:59.4 seconds. He did what one former record holder, Glenn Cunningham, said was impossible for a human being. This team was so inspiring that their record was broken in forty-six days. Then, it was beaten again and again. Today, over nine hundred people have run a mile in under four minutes. Roger Bannister and his "drafters" created a paradigm shift for sprinters around the world.

WHO ARE YOUR DRAFTERS?

Drafters are people who are faster than you and catalyze your growth.

Each January, I enlist "drafters" to help me adapt and grow in five or six categories that I choose. They are either people in my industry that I deem faster than me, or they are people who've mastered a skill I need. I meet with them, with a tablet of questions, and they invest in me their insight and ideas. Tim Tassopoulos is my drafter in focus. John Maxwell is a drafter for me in leadership. Steve Moore is a drafter for me in digesting data and applying it.

Drafters are people who are ahead of you and inspire you to get better.

Sometimes, my drafters are people that I don't know personally, but whom I can watch and listen to regularly. They are people whose careers overlap with mine, meaning at least part of what they do parallels what I do, and they model for me what's around the next bend. Often, they are more experienced in an area and have moved beyond current protocols or processes to get ahead. In many ways, Chris Carneal does this for me; Brené Brown does this for me; Carol Dweck does this for me; Jonathan Haidt does this for me.

Drafters are people who want you to win and cooperate to help you to succeed.

I joined John Maxwell's staff in 1983 and served alongside of him for twenty years. Every step of the way, he was a drafter for me. He set the pace, clarified the vision we were targeting, and usually modeled the strategy or philosophy we'd use to reach our goals. Even after I launched my own nonprofit, John has been a drafter. He was the first person to make a donation, and every time I meet with him I have no doubt he wants me to win. I have been very fortunate to have such a person in my life.

WHAT DOES TIMELESS LOOK LIKE?

Allow me to remind you of Larry Merlo's decision in 2014. Larry is the CEO of CVS Health drugstores. That year, he was asked why CVS (and for that matter all major drugstores) sold cigarettes, when they claimed to be about health and wellness. This question forced Larry to review his pharmacy's purpose statement over the next several days. As he considered it, he felt CVS was at an impasse. Their purpose was about *helping people on the path to better health.* Cigarettes did not align with that path, even though it generated billions of dollars of sales every year. Shortly

What are your next steps to remain timely?

afterward, Larry met with his board and his executive team with the crazy idea that their chain should stop selling cigarettes. He felt it was hypocritical.

Needless to say, his decision caused quite a stir. While everyone saw this misalignment, they saw more clearly what this would do to income and profit margins. Would stakeholders drop out? Would customers who bought cigarettes stop shopping at CVS? It was a risk, but Larry prevailed, and the chain stopped selling the multibillion-dollar line of products.

For Larry Merlo, it was about remaining timeless. He was being true to their purpose, which had been carefully crafted decades earlier. If he'd turned a blind eye, he wouldn't be true to his own integrity or to the purpose of the organization, which he stewarded. His plumb line was clear; CVS and other pharmacies had become crooked.

What happened as a result?

Against all odds, sales held steady at many CVS stores. They discovered that some of their smoking customers just stopped smoking and many other people, hearing of the decision, decided to start shopping at CVS, to support such a courageous decision. They literally drove past other drugstores to patronize CVS. CVS continued to grow.

Uncommon leaders change the report card and customers tend to give them an A.

Summary of this paradox

TIMELESS	TIMELY
1. Ensures you don't get sidetracked.	1. Ensures you make progress.
2. Maintains your moral compass.	2. Maintains your future focus.
3. Values remain central.	3. Improvement remains central.

4. Makes your team feel safe.	4. Makes your team feel relevant.
5. A bridge to your past heritage.	5. A bridge to your hopeful possibilities.

Practicing the paradox of a timely and timeless leader

This chapter has already offered ideas for practicing this paradox. Below is an acronym to guide you in your "timely" and "timeless" lifestyle. Each time you create a new product or service, ensure that it's a thing of BEAUTY. As you embrace timeless values that serve as your "plumb line," consider this gauge for your future offerings:

Creating a thing of BEAUTY

B—Better. It isn't just different. It is superior in meeting a need or satisfying a want.

E—Entrepreneurial. It is new and fresh and feels like you're the first one to offer it.

A—Adaptable. It is a product or service customers can customize and personalize.

U—Unique. It's nothing like what's already available; it stands apart from competition.

T—Timely. It fills a hole in real time, being relevant for the moment people are living.

Y—Yearly. It is renewable, creating ongoing revenue through annual upgrades and updates.

Just over fifty years ago, Walt Disney gathered his inner circle to inform them of his idea to build "Disneyland," which he claimed would be known as the "happiest place on earth." Walt's vision was clear and focused. As the team began to get excited about the vision, however, one of the members asked, "Who are you gonna get to build it?" Confidently, Walt responded, "I know exactly who I want to build it. Find me the man who helped put the US Navy back in the Pacific, after the bombing of Pearl Harbor. I figure he can do it."

It didn't take long for Walt's team to identify this man. His name was Joe Fowler. Admiral Joe Fowler. Retired admiral Joe Fowler. When Disney showed up at Fowler's door, challenging him to build a theme park, Joe laughed. "You don't understand. I'm retired. I'm through." But after placing pictures on the wall and speaking in great detail about the feel, look, smell, sound, and even taste of the park—Walt got Joe to buy in. He stepped out of retirement and oversaw Disneyland's construction.

Years later, Disney World was set to be created—and can you guess who was hired to supervise the project? That's right, Joe Fowler, at seventy-seven years old. When the Disney team approached him a second time, they got the same response: "I'm retired. I'm through." But as pictures were posted and vision was cast for their biggest project yet, Joe couldn't help but buy in again.

Ten years later, with the building of EPCOT, Disney executives again asked Joe Fowler to lead the construction. This eighty-seven-year-old retiree sighed and tried to turn them down once again. "You don't understand. I'm retired. I'm through." But everyone knew, Joe was the man. After the Disney team communicated clear, focused vision, Joe couldn't help but abandon retirement again and participate in a third project.

What a perfect illustration of the energy accompanying good vision. Joe's coined response of, "I'm retired. I'm through," changed into, "You don't have to die till you want to." Fowler admitted as a retiree that he was energized by both the ageless values of Walt Disney and the future focus of what could be achieved tomorrow. It's enough to give energy to anyone.

THINK IT THROUGH, TALK IT OVER

- Do you know leaders who balance "timely" and "timeless" well?
- Which of these two qualities do you lean toward naturally? Why is the other hard?
- What are the "plumb lines" for your leadership and organization?
- What must you do to improve practicing this paradox?

A NEW KIND OF LEADER

I mourn the fact that, far too often today, self-serving leaders who participate in scandals have become common. We entered the twenty-first century with formal charges brought against companies like Enron, Tyco, and Worldcom for corruption, conspiracy, grand larceny, and falsifying records.

Enron shares were worth over $90 at their peak but plummeted to $0.67 immediately after the scandal was revealed. If that wasn't enough, that same year the accounting firm Arthur Andersen was convicted of obstruction of justice for shredding documents related to its audit of Enron. This is what we often expect from corporate leaders. It's sad that we need whistleblowers to keep an eye on them because they won't watch themselves.

How did this happen?

The economist Milton Friedman offered a "report card" for business in the 1970s. He taught that the responsibility of business leaders is to *maximize profits within the boundaries of the law.*[1] He did not intend to, but, with this definition, Friedman gave business leaders permission to set a very low standard. It's why drugstores can sell cigarettes even though their purpose statement is about improving the health of their customers. Those stores may say they value health, but really they value profit margins. Consider this: when the *Titanic* was built, it was larger than any other ship and needed more lifeboats. The law, however, required only enough lifeboats for a typical ferry, which was one-fourth of what they'd need. So, what did they do? They stocked the *Titanic* with only 25 percent of what it really needed. When it struck an iceberg, all but one-fourth of the people aboard died. They broke no laws.

While I believe in a free market economy, it only works over the long haul with uncommon leaders who prioritize people and adding value to their communities over generating income.

If you lead a public company, it is difficult to live by such values and sustain trust because increasing revenue is more important to shareholders than doing what's right. Leaders are obsessed with one report card: generating more income. It's the standard of business and why so many corporate leaders will hide scandalous decisions (as Enron did). Their work is about:

- Shareholders, not customers.
- Short-term, not long-term, thinking.
- Generating revenue, not adding value.

These are common leaders, not uncommon ones, who possess a finite mindset vs. an infinite one, according to history professor James P. Carse.[2]

Emerging in our day, however, are uncommon leaders, like the ones we've discussed in this book. They maneuver past the obsession over profits today—by taking the long view. They know that income will follow uncommon leadership. It's what Bob Iger did when he displayed confidence and humility. It's what Sara Blakely did as she utilized her vision and her blind spots. It's how Martin Luther King Jr. leveraged his visibility and invisibility. It's what Truett Cathy did as he modeled stubborn and open-minded leadership. It's how Mother Teresa led in a personal and collective manner. It's how Angela Ahrendts remained a teacher and a learner. It's how Harriet Tubman demonstrated high standards and gracious forgiveness. It's how Walt Disney led in a timely and timeless fashion.

Each of these people represents a new kind of leader.

I see this new kind of leader surfacing across almost every industry—in business, athletics, nonprofits, healthcare, education, and churches. They are unique individuals who have "gotten over themselves" in view of a bigger picture. They change the way they pursue their goals. And they find a way to leverage the particular chemistry of their team and combine it with their own unique strengths to hit a target.

THE SHIFT TO THIS NEW KIND OF LEADER

Old-style leaders appear invincible; fully in control and knowing all the answers. New-style leaders practice the paradoxes we've discussed in this book. They read nuances as they interact with people; they are emotionally available and socially aware of their surroundings; they admit mistakes and weaknesses without losing an ounce of respect. To use Generation Z's language, they are "woke" but in a fuller sense of the term. They're fully human yet push human potential to its limits in the pursuit of a worthwhile mission. They're emotionally secure and tend to cultivate secure environments.

The reason they're authentic and admit mistakes?

They know that being real and acknowledging errors doesn't cause others to respect them less. Others respect them all the more. It's yet another paradox. Further, these leaders also know that subordinates pattern themselves after their leaders. If we leaders don't admit our errors, neither will our teams. They avoid the cultural norm of hiding, lying, and faking. They refuse to allow a culture of rationalization and cover-up because they model transparency for others. People do what people see.

One early example of this new kind of leader is Army General Tommy Franks. Twenty years ago, General Franks led the attack on the Taliban in Afghanistan in response to the September 11, 2001, attacks on the World Trade Center and the Pentagon. He also oversaw the 2003 invasion of Iraq. When asked a complex question at a press conference, reporters were surprised when he didn't have a succinct answer and admitted that he didn't know the answer. Instead of the typical "I'll get back to you" response, Franks was quick to acknowledge that not everything is knowable. This was a refreshing admission from a military officer.[3]

Have you observed any similar shifts in leadership style?

Two decades ago, numerous thought leaders began spotting these leaders and using new language to describe them. By 2006, we began to see a shift in how leaders managed their teams. A tipping point was reached in many organizations as authenticity overtook pretense. I believe this shift took place organically as leaders recognized society had migrated from the "modern world" to the "postmodern world." It was, in essence, a shift from the scientific age to the relationship age.

SCIENTIFIC AGE	RELATIONSHIP AGE
1. Technical skills.	1. People skills.
2. Command and control.	2. Connect and collaborate.
3. Motivated by competition.	3. Motivated by compassion.
4. Gathering facts.	4. Finding meaning.
5. Focus is to sell a product.	5. Focus is to solve a problem.
6. Hierarchy (top down).	6. Circular (egalitarian).
7. Never let 'em see you sweat.	7. Be authentic and vulnerable.
8. Mostly about IQ.	8. Mostly about EQ.

This is not to say that the technical skills, the desire to sell a product, or a high IQ are nonexistent in today's relationship age.

I am simply saying the focus and priorities have shifted because what's scarce today is not intelligence (even artificial intelligence) but rather healthy relationships; those marked by high emotional and social intelligence.

THE EVOLUTION OF LEADERSHIP OVER HUMAN HISTORY

Let's take a moment and reflect on how we got here. How did leadership begin? How did individuals amass authority over time? How is it that people let one person have power over a crowd or a country? Below is a quick summary of how leadership evolved over the centuries.

How leaders won their right to lead through history

- Divine right (Common throughout ancient history). It comes from God, so no one could debate the decisions or competence of the leader.
- Familial right (Common in the medieval age). It comes from birthright, which often created distant, domineering styles in monarchies.
- Electoral right (Common in the enlightenment age). It comes from a social contract as people vote and select leaders to represent them.
- Competence right (Common through the modern age). It comes from recognition that a certain person is best gifted to run point and guide others.
- Connection right (Becoming more common today). It comes from trusting relationships within a community ignited by a wise, inclusive leader.

Allow me to furnish an allegory to illustrate this evolution.

Dorothy's Way

One of my favorite memories growing up as a kid was watching the movie *The Wizard of Oz* on TV. It came on every year. We'd pop popcorn and sit around as a family watching Dorothy, the scarecrow, the tin man, and the cowardly lion make their way to the Emerald City in the Land of Oz. I still enjoy the movie. It's a classic.

Today, however, I watch it through a different lens. As I sat with my own kids years ago, I learned new skills from Dorothy—watching the film from a leadership perspective. (I know it sounds crazy, but I seem to find leadership principles in almost every movie I see, from *Dumb and Dumber* to *Anchorman.*) This time, my leadership discovery came from a very ordinary girl from Kansas who would not claim to be a leader at all.

As I observe trends in our culture, it seems to me that there is a cry for this new kind of leader. We've moved through various leadership styles over the last fifty years—and many of them can be seen in this classic movie. Reflect on the characters and note the leaders we meet:

1. The Wicked Witch of the West—She has her cronies, but they follow because she forces them to do so. She leads through *manipulation.* She coerces them. People dislike her greatly, and when she finally melts even her followers celebrate.
2. The Wizard of Oz—He is the all-powerful leader, who leads through *intimidation.* He comes across as superior. People are afraid of him. He is all-wise and in control—the kind of leader we tend to imagine is the best one for the job.
3. Dorothy—She is an unlikely leader who doesn't have all the answers, but invites her friends on a journey, discovers their gifts, walks with them

> rather than insist on being up front, and runs point as they pursue their goal together.

At first glance, Dorothy appears all wrong as a model of leadership. I am certain she never felt like she was a leader. At the time, she was the wrong gender (female) and the wrong age (young) for what people might have expected in a leader. Instead of being a person who has all the solutions and knows exactly what to do next—she is herself on a journey, a seeker, often bewildered and vulnerable. Yet she is determined to get her team, made up of a scarecrow, a tin man, and a cowardly lion, to the wizard, where they can find what they're looking for. Armed with this resolve, she walks down the yellow brick road on a journey of discovery, with her newfound friends. No one expects her to have all the answers. They don't want a "sage on the stage," but a "guide on the side" to help them reach their goal.

Now contrast Dorothy with the Great Wizard himself. Frequently, many of us avoid leadership positions because we hold an image of a leader in our heads that looks much like the Wizard of Oz. Remember how he introduces himself? "I am Oz, the great and powerful!" In other words—just look to me for any answers you need. I'm in charge. Because few believe they're really this good, they conclude they must not have what it takes to be a leader. But do you remember what happens in the end? Little Toto (Dorothy's dog) pulls back the curtain to reveal that the great Wizard is a rather normal guy hiding behind an imposing image. This all-powerful leader was, in a sense, exposed as a fraud. He didn't have the answers after all. It was all a front.

When you think of Dorothy, the picture is so different. She introduces herself to the Wizard as "Dorothy—the small and the meek." Instead of sitting confidently in a control booth, she's stuck in a predicament—still a little frazzled from the tornado, far from home, needing to find the way. As she begins her journey to the Emerald City, she finds other characters who share her goal, and her earnestness, her compassion, and her spark of determination galvanize them into a team. She ends up coming to realize that they each had the brains, the heart, and the courage they were seeking, already inside of them. Dorothy isn't able to avoid all the pitfalls or dangers; she doesn't protect them from all the threats—but she encourages them, and she doesn't give up. Her passion holds strong and fosters the same resolve in each of her team members. Dorothy has so invested in them that the lion, the scarecrow, and the tin man all decide they are going to get to that Wizard to help Dorothy—even if they don't get what they wanted! Now that's loyalty.

This is a picture of a new kind of leader. It's a team effort and no one person is the only star. While Dorothy owned her mission, each person on the team took the lead at appropriate times. Each one stood up for the others before it was over. Each had gifts and abilities. Dorothy simply ran point. Management guru Peter Drucker notes that these uncommon leaders must be okay without having all the answers. They must be humble enough to seek wisdom from others, yet courageous enough to act when it's time. Drucker suggests that "the leader of the past was a person who knew how to tell. The leader of the future will be a person who knows how to ask."

This is still another one of my *Habitudes*® that illustrate leadership today. I believe I see these Dorothy-type leaders in more and more places. They've transported themselves from a predictable, flat, black-and-white world (in Kansas) to a zany, full-color world (in Oz). It is unpredictable, sometimes illogical, and often confusing.

Frank Baum's story *The Wizard of Oz* was intended to be a sort of parable for us. You likely recall he wrote it as a commentary on the economic and political times at the turn of the twentieth century. The scarecrow represented the farmers who were perceived as uneducated; they were folks without a brain. The tin man represented businessmen, who didn't seem to have any heart. The cowardly lion symbolized the politician William Jennings Bryan who Baum felt lacked the courage to stand up to the wrongs in Washington, DC. The wizard symbolized the federal government—who didn't really have the answers everyone sought. And Dorothy represented the average citizen who showed her friends they had what it took to reach their dreams. They just needed to work as a team under a different leadership style. Frank Baum was revealing to us a new kind of leader.

THE EVOLUTION OF LEADERSHIP IN OUR LIFETIME

In this book, we've examined eight leadership paradoxes that make leaders outstanding. I believe they're essential today because leadership approaches have evolved over the last seventy years. The times have demanded this change, as people have recalibrated with the culture. Each new population of team members seeks out a different kind of leader who matches the times. Those who flourish today will embrace the paradoxes we've discussed.

THE EVOLUTION OF LEADERSHIP STYLES

Leadership is a little like a dance. Leaders partner up with teams, and they initiate but their people must reciprocate. It is dynamic, requiring leaders to be self-aware and socially aware of what's happening between them. And while the mission may remain the same, the methods may need to change to stay in step. The acceptable style changes with the times. The way we led in 1950 looks different than it does today. Let's take a look at this evolution of approaches:

1950s	1960s–1970s	1980s	1990s	2000s	TODAY
Military Commander	Chief Executive Officer	The Entrepreneur	The Coach	The Connector	The Poet-Gardener

1. **Military Commander.** This style was about authority and submission. They valued loyalty.
2. **Chief Executive Officer.** This style was about vision and progress. They valued productivity.
3. **The Entrepreneur.** This style was about being first and best. They valued innovation.
4. **The Coach.** This style was about teamwork and morale. They valued collaboration.
5. **The Connector.** This style was about alignment of individuals. They valued connection.
6. **The Poet-Gardener.** This style is about interpretation and development. They value empowerment and growth.

As we proceed into the third decade of the twenty-first century, I see a new kind of leader on the horizon. It is a leader who's in touch with the postmodern world in which we live. This leader combines many of the strengths of the last four styles. In addition, he or she is secure enough to build relationships with their teams and drive the process toward getting the desired result. We'll call this type of leader a poet and a gardener.

This new generation of leaders doesn't enter their position assuming they have all the answers. They surround themselves with a team of other leaders (not just a team of players, but a leadership team). This inner circle is optimally diverse in their strengths and perspectives—but not in their values and vision. As this team meets to discuss ideas, the Poet-Gardener listens and adds, then ultimately puts words to the ideas that seem to be surfacing in the group.

The *leader-poets* are discerning of the culture and the ideas that emerge from others, not just themselves. In the same way we enjoy a poem because the writer expresses what we're feeling and thinking in words, this leader summarizes big-picture ideas with clarity and poignance. They synthesize and extrapolate thoughts;

then they champion the best one, even if it is not their own. At this point, they become a wordsmith who articulates the idea until the entire team owns it. They give language to the ideas and feelings the people possess. While the *leader-poet* has many good ideas, they don't pretend to think up all the answers, and the pressure is off of them to do so. They are communicators of the best ideas, regardless of the source. They recognize that people no longer rely on a leader to gain information—it's accessible to all. Needless to say, these leaders are attractive to a new workforce who long to be part of creating vision and determining direction. People support what they help create.

The *leader-gardeners* are people-developers. Just as the primary function of a gardener is to cultivate the soil, pull the weeds and create an environment where plants can grow, the leader-gardeners see their primary function as developing their people, not simply doing business. They're equippers. They see themselves as mentors to their team. Relationship is inherent in this style of leadership. Employees will want to stick around because they see the value in staying. They will not only help the organization get to the goal; they will grow in the process. The employee doesn't merely feel like a number or a cog in the wheel. They are not "used" by their boss—they are developed, and they become useful in the process.

The key values of this kind of leader are empowerment and growth. First, as they *connect* with their people, they lend their power to them. This creates the culture within their organization. People have agency. Secondly, they value *growth*—not just organizationally but for each person in it. They resource everyone for personal and professional growth. They lead out of shared ownership. Everyone owns the vision and flourishes as they move toward it.

I believe this is the attractive leader of today. I'm not saying all the others will die out. Based on temperament and generation, other styles will remain, and some will do well because of the strength of the leader's personality and vision. But the style today's new generation of employees will want is the Poet-Gardener. This leader can adapt to the need of the moment.

Characteristics of a Poet-Gardener

The qualities we value in leaders tend to remain constant (integrity, purpose, wisdom, etc.) but the style or approach is different. Leaders change the steps in the dance and embrace the paradoxes in this book. The healthy Poet-Gardener possesses these characteristics:

1. They are highly relational.
2. They interpret culture well.
3. They are emotionally secure.
4. They share ownership freely.
5. They empower others.
6. They're comfortable with uncertainty.
7. They listen and foster self-discovery.
8. They embrace the role of a mentor.
9. They're less formal in structure.
10. They're driven by service more than ego.

Ultimately, because they read situations before they lead them, they practice paradoxical leadership as a norm. They are both confident and humble. They leverage both their vision and their blind spots. They balance visibility and invisibility. You get the idea.

THE CHOICE IN FRONT OF US

The choice in front of us is to go first. To become vulnerable. To not expect any team member to initiate change and transparency, but to risk it ourselves.

This is scary because our world is volatile, uncertain, complex, and ambiguous, as I suggested in the first chapter. We'd rather hide instead of running out into the open where everyone can see us. We find it more comfortable to be a "guard dog" who is protecting, barking, and suspicious of outsiders. Their job is to protect. "Guide dogs," on the other hand, go first, model the way, and take those who may not see what's ahead with them on a journey. Their job is to partner.

In what ways have you embodied the qualities of a Poet-Gardener leader?

Leaders and teams tend to protect naturally more than partner. Although humans are wired for both protecting and partnering, most of us are conditioned to be guard dogs first. We are watchful, holding our cards close to our chest. We don't want to become too vulnerable when our environment may be unsafe. Much like a guard dog, we "sniff" around for social cues to how to respond.

Why do we do this so naturally and predictably?

It's quite simple. The amygdala is the part of our brain that serves as our primeval vigilance device, constantly scanning any and all environments. It lights up when in threatening or uncertain social settings, sending the signal: *fight, flight, or freeze.* Biologically, we've needed it over the centuries to survive. The amygdala develops earlier than our prefrontal cortex, which later helps us make more calculated, rational judgments. You could call the amygdala our "first responder."

A few years ago, I consulted with a business team that struggled to collaborate. Each department in this company needed to work closely together, depending on each other to get their projects done. Unfortunately, these people never opened up, distrusted the others, and refused to do anything beyond the minimum requirement. As I met with individual team members, it became clear that the root of the distrust was Amelia, a person who'd been hired eighteen months earlier. As I met with Amelia, she was able to identify her trust issues and why she withheld information from others. A man who served in another department vividly reminded her of her former husband. This man looked like him and acted with the same mannerisms as her "ex." While Amelia knew this man was not the same person who had hurt her, she had to make a constant effort to overcome the "fight, flight, or freeze" reactions her brain prompted her to make.

The good news is the amygdala can be conditioned to fend off instincts. Neural pathways can be developed to trust, to be transparent, and to collaborate. It lights up differently when safety cues are sent: when someone cares, understands, and empathizes.

This requires intentional effort. Someone has to initiate.

I'll never forget the day I was in a frightening plane crash in New Zealand. Our private plane was attempting to land on a field with a wooded area on two sides, and homes on another. Our pilot was not instrument rated, and when he realized his landing attempt was not going to work, he took the plane back up to circle the field and try our landing again. As we surged into the air (to miss the trees), our engine stalled, our pilot panicked, and we dropped 120 feet to the ground. We were all beaten up and bloodied, but we all survived the crash. Needless to say, however, my horrible memories of that day made it tough for me every time I had to board a plane throughout that next year. When I did, I relived that air crash every time our plane experienced turbulence. I still have marks, physically and emotionally, from that experience.

I knew, however, I had to avoid the survival zone. I would need to ride airplanes again, just to get home. I would want to speak again, which is why I was there in the first place. So, I fought my instincts to seek safety. Since I was damaged less than my comrades, they were life-flighted off to the hospital while I stayed back and rested, preparing for my speaking event that night.

It became my opportunity to influence.

While I rested in a home nearby, reporters showed up from the two national television networks in New Zealand. They sought to interview someone who saw the plane crash. The homeowners smiled and said, "Saw the plane crash? We've got someone in the back room who was *in* the plane crash!" When they discovered I was up to it, I hobbled out to the backyard, they leaned me up against a tree (since I wasn't standing very straight at the time), and asked me to speak to the people of New Zealand.

It was my chance to be a guide dog—and influence three million Kiwis.

Was I scared? Of course I was. I am human like you. Was my amygdala sending signals to run and hide? You bet it was. That would have been safer. Was the situation out of my control? Yes, except for my response. Leaders don't earn their right to influence by running and hiding.

Our world needs leaders who are secure enough to assume the role of "guide dogs." This not only means we take initiative with strategies to fulfill our mission, but with our transparency about our weaknesses. The signals people need from leaders are:

- I am a human, even before I am a professional.
- I feel for you and recognize your plight.
- I am with you. I am for you. I have your back.

According to author Daniel Coyle, belonging works from the *outside in,* not the inside out. This means, people unconsciously search for cues (from others) before they jump in and become "guide dogs." Most people need others to signal to them they're safe before they stop wondering: "What do I need to do to survive?" When in this kind of transparent environment:

- You're less concerned about your status.
- You are not as worried about who gets credit for ideas.
- You are more prone to try harder and sacrifice for the whole.

"The moment you're part of a group, the amygdala tunes in to who's in that group and starts intensely tracking them. These people were strangers before; now they're important to you. It's such a powerful switch; a total reconfiguration of the entire motivational decision-making system. The whole dynamic changes," says Jay Van Bavel, neuroscientist at New York University.

So, what's the key? Vulnerability and transparency.

THE SECRET TO AN EXTRAORDINARY EXPERIENCE

The secret is—someone has to start. Leaders must learn to say things like, "I just made a huge mistake." Or, "Anyone have any ideas for our next step?" Or, "I apologize. Would you forgive me?" On a team, members—and especially leaders—must assume this posture:

1. I must go first.
2. I must model transparency.
3. I must be vulnerable.
4. I must trust.

I remember the day our leadership team at Growing Leaders chose to leave our work for an entire day so our staff could help a team member move her possessions out of her apartment and get to safety from an unhealthy relationship. We generated no revenue that day, but boy did they bond as they rescued a teammate. Uncommon leadership.

When our leadership team saw we would not reach our numbers in the summer of 2020, as COVID-19 took its toll on our organization, they knew it meant no one would get a bonus. Before any options were placed on the table, our leaders instantly chose to surrender their bonuses so the rest of the team could receive theirs. Uncommon leadership.

My career began more than forty years ago. I have met these uncommon leaders again and again and watched them produce extraordinary results with teams as they led in a new way. They balanced paradoxes because their personal "report card" was not merely about money.

It's people like Dan Price who decided the disparity in salaries on his team was causing hardship for some and determined that everyone—including him—would make the same income.

Or like Nelson Mandela who, as the first black president of South Africa, didn't make "black supremacy" the issue of his leadership, but worked to bring races together to beat apartheid.

Or Oprah Winfrey who, in the 1990s, when talk shows like Jerry Springer dominated the ratings with trashy topics, promised to keep her show respectful and about generosity and faith.

My challenge to you is to join their ranks.

I believe our world needs changing, and this is one primary way to get that done. Leading in this way captures the attention of everyone and accomplishes what common leadership cannot. We have a chance to move the needle, one paradox at a time.

It will change your brand. It will change your customers. It will change your team.

In 1984, the band U2 recorded the song "(Pride) In the Name of Love." It reflected their mission: to be a voice for social justice. The song, which was about Dr. Martin Luther King Jr., was written as a part of the movement to secure a holiday in his name. The musicians of U2 were more than a band; they were a team. They stood together, through thick and thin, even when in conflict.

As they performed the song repeatedly throughout that year, lead singer Bono one day received a death threat. An anonymous letter from a white supremacist said that if Bono sang that song in his city—a bullet would be lodged in his head before the song was over. The band met and everyone believed it was unwise to include the song in their playlist that night. It wasn't worth it. Everyone agreed—that is, except for Bono, who reminded them of their mission. He was determined to sing that song, come what may. This leader modeled vulnerability even at the risk of his life that night.

Bono later said in an interview, he closed his eyes as he began to sing the lyrics, knowing it might be the last song he ever sang. But surprisingly, he continued to sing, longer and longer. He wasn't sure why the bullets weren't flying. When he finally opened his eyes—he saw what was happening. One by one, fellow band members were taking turns stepping in front of him . . . to take the bullet.

Sounds like a team I'd like to be a part of. Sounds like some uncommon leaders to me.

ACKNOWLEDGMENTS

Every author knows a book is a team effort. The people who were willing to support me in the creation of this book are many. Here are some key people below:

John Maxwell—who believes in me to a fault. He always finds ways to express his excitement over my ideas and loans me his influence so I can broadcast them.

Matt Litton—who served as a content and line editor for each chapter. Thanks, Matt, for your input on the ideas and how they are laid out. You made this book better.

Andrew McPeak—who served as a reader and editor. He knows me well and ensured the ideas I hoped to communicate were clear and digestible. Thanks, Andrew, for your input.

The John Maxwell Company Leaders—who agreed to get behind this book and promote it to their coaches and tribe. You have been longtime friends I don't deserve.

The Growing Leaders team—who listened in when I first taught these paradoxes and not only discussed them but offered feedback to make them better. Thanks for that feedback, GL.

The Phase Family Center—for providing quiet space for me to get away and write. This project would have been difficult to pull off without that space. Thank you.

Andy Stanley—who heard about these paradoxes and immediately offered platforms to share them with his North Point teams, the Leadership Lab, and his podcast.

The HarperCollins Leadership team—who got behind me when they didn't know me and chose to support this book idea as the first installment of the John Maxwell Imprint.

My bride of forty years, Pam—who always stands by me, living her life with a strong bias for me. Thanks, PJ, for being a safety net for decades. I love you.

ENDNOTES

Paradoxical Leadership in a Complex Age

1. "2019 September CEO Turnover Report," Challenger, Gray, and Christmas, Inc., http://www.challengergray.com/press/press-releases/2019-september-ceo-turnover-report-highest-ytd-quarterly-totals-record.
2. Rebecca Aydin and Allana Akhtar, "The 37 most dramatic CEO exits in 2019," *Business Insider*, December 23, 2019, https://www.businessinsider.com/biggest-ceo-departures-wework-juul-ebay-warner-bros-metlife-2019-10.
3. Polina Marinova, "The Great CEO Exodus of 2020," *Fortune*, February 26, 2020, https://fortune.com/2020/02/26/the-great-ceo-exodus-of-2020/.
4. Scott Gregory, March 30, 2018, "The Most Common Type of Incompetent Leader," *Harvard Business Review*, https://hbr.org/2018/03/the-most-common-type-of-incompetent-leader.
5. Czeisler et al., "Mental Health, Substance Use, and Suicidal Ideation During the COVID-19 Pandemic—United States, June 24–30, 2020," Morbidity and Mortality Weekly Report, Centers for Disease Control and Prevention, August 14, 2020, https://www.cdc.gov/mmwr/volumes/69/wr/mm6932a1.htm.
6. Rick Nason, *It's Not Complicated: The Art and Science of Complexity in Business* (Toronto, Canada: University of Toronto Press, 2017).
7. Adam Saenz, *The EQ Intervention* (Austin, TX: Greenleaf Book Group Press, 2020).
8. Kristen Bialik and Richard Fry, "Millennial Life: How Young Adulthood Compares Today with Prior Generations," Pew Research Center, February 14, 2019, https://www.pewsocialtrends.org/essay/millennial-life-how-young-adulthood-today-compares-with-prior-generations/.
9. Greg Evans, "Psychologists Say More and More Young People Are Entitled," *Independent*, August 1, 2017, https://www.indy100.com/article/young-people-entitlement-disappointed-narcissism-psychology-research-7867961.

10. Mellissah Smith, "We Are Exposed to 10,000 Brand Messages a Day," *Marketing Eye*, September 24, 2018, https://www.marketingeye.com.au/marketing-blog/we-are-exposed-to-10-000-brand-messages-per-day-here-s-how-to-make-yours-stick.html.
11. David Rock, *Quiet Leadership* (New York: HarperCollins, 2006).
12. Travis Bradberry and Jean Greaves, *Emotional Intelligence 2.0* (San Diego: TalentSmart, 2009), 7–8.
13. Bradberry and Greaves, *Emotional Intelligence*, 17.
14. Bradberry and Greaves, *Emotional Intelligence*, 21.
15. Jonathan Haidt, *The Righteous Mind* (New York: Knopf, 2012).

Paradox One

1. Robert Iger, *The Ride of a Lifetime* (New York: Random House Publishers, 2019), 36.
2. Iger, *Ride of a Lifetime*, 36.
3. Iger, *Ride of a Lifetime*, 36–37.
4. Iger, *Ride of a Lifetime*, 37.
5. Dacher Keltner, *The Power Paradox: How We Gain and Lose Influence* (New York: Penguin/Random House Books, 2016).
6. Dan Reiland, *Confident Leader!: Become One, Stay One* (Nashville: Thomas Nelson Publishers, 2020).
7. Jim C. Collins, *Good to Great: Why Some Companies Make the Leap . . . and Others Don't* (New York: HarperCollins, 2001).
8. Daniel Coyle, *Culture Code* (New York: Bantam Books, 2018).
9. Coyle, *Culture Code.*
10. Tim Elmore, *Habitudes: The Art of Connecting with Others* (Atlanta: Poet Gardner Publishers, 2006).
11. Peter Skillman, peterskillmandesign.com.
12. Peter Skillman, peterskillmandesign.com.
13. Patrick Lencioni, The Table Group, Inc., 250 Lafayette Circle, Suite 300, Lafayette, CA 94549.

Paradox Two

1. Triston V. Sanders, "Spanx Creator Sara Blakely Makes the World a Better Place, One Butt at a Time," *Tallahassee*, July 20, 2012, https://www.tallahasseemagazine.com/spanx-creator-sara-blakely-makes-the-world-a-better-place-one-butt-at-a-time/.
2. Melia Patria, "Spanx Founder Reveals How to Build a Billion-Dollar Business," ABC News, abcnews.go.com, November 29, 2012.
3. *Atlanta Business Chronicle*, "Sara Blakely No. 91 on *Forbes*' 'The World's 100 Most Powerful Women' List," May 26, 2015, https://www.bizjournals.com/atlanta/news/2015/05/26/sara-blakely-no-91-on-forbes-the-world-s-100-most.html.

4. Liane Hansen, "The Race for Flight," October 19, 2003, NPR, npr.org, https://www.npr.org/templates/story/story.php?storyId=1469463.
5. "Victim of Wikipedia: Microsoft to Shut Down Encarta," *Forbes*, March 30, 2009, www.forbes.com › 2009/03/30 › microsoft-encarta-wiki.
6. Dan Schwabel, "Why 'Gen Z' May Be More Entrepreneurial Than 'Gen Y,'" *Entrepreneur*, February 3, 2014, https://www.entrepreneur.com/article/231048.
7. Burt Helm, "Meet the Best-Connected 21-Year-Old in the World, *Inc.*, July/August, 2011, https://www.inc.com/magazine/201107/ankur-jain-the-best-connected-21-year-old-in-the-world.html.
8. Tim Elmore, *Habitudes for Career Ready Students* (Atlanta: Poet Gardener Publishers, 2015).
9. Marisa Meltzer, "How Emily Weiss Grew Glossier from Millennial Catnip to Billion-Dollar Juggernaut," *Vanity Fair*, October, 2010, https://www.vanityfair.com/style/2019/10/how-emily-weiss-grew-glossier-from-millennial-catnip-to-billion-dollar-juggernaut.
10. Aditya Shukla "The Einstellung Effect: Why Experts Lack Creativity and Problem-Solving Skills," *Cognition Today*, July 12, 2019, https://cognitiontoday.com/2019/07/the-einstellung-effect-why-experts-lack-creativity-and-problem-solving-skills/.

Paradox Three

1. Martin Luther King Jr., "An Autobiography of Religious Development," The Martin Luther King Jr. Research and Education Institute. Stanford University. Archived from the original on December 18, 2014, https://kinginstitute.stanford.edu/king-papers/documents/autobiography-religious-development.
2. Marshall Frady, *Martin Luther King Jr.: A Life* (New York: Penguin, 2002).
3. Manning Marable, Immanuel Ness, and Joseph Wilson, eds., *Race and Labor Matters in the New U.S. Economy* (Lanham, MD: Rowman & Littlefield, 2006), 47.
4. Gary Wills, *Certain Trumpets* (New York: Simon and Schuster, 1994), 218.
5. Martin Luther King Jr., *The Papers of Martin Luther King, Jr., Volume One*, eds., Carson, Luker, and Russell (Oakland: University of California Press, 1992), 47.
6. Thomas F. Jackson, *From Civil Rights to Human Rights: Martin Luther King Jr. and the Struggle for Economic Justice* (Philadelphia: University of Pennsylvania Press, 2006).
7. Coretta Scott King, "The Meaning of The King Holiday," The King Center. Archived from the original on May 14, 2013. Retrieved August 22, 2012.
8. Bill Hudson, https://en.wikipedia.org/wiki/Bill_Hudson_(photographer).

9. David Garrow, *Bearing the Cross: Martin Luther King, Jr., and the Southern Christian Leadership Conference* (New York: Morrow, 1986), 246.
10. *Unto a Good Land: A History of the American People, Volume 2,* Harrell et al., eds. (Grand Rapids, MI: William B. Eerdmans Publishing, 2005), 1055.
11. Mind Tools, https://www.mindtools.com/mnemlsty.html.
12. Lou Solomon, "The Top Complaints from Employees About Their Leaders," *Harvard Business Review,* June 24, 2015, https://hbr.org/2015/06/the-top-complaints-from-employees-about-their-leaders.
13. Skogstad, et al., "The Relative Effects of Constructive, Laissez-Faire, and Tyrannical Leadership on Subordinate Job Satisfaction," *Zeitschrift für Psychologie* 222 (2014) 221–232, https://econtent.hogrefe.com/doi/abs/10.1027/2151-2604/a000189.

Paradox Four

1. Matthew McCreary, "Chick-fil-A Makes More Per Restaurant Than McDonald's, Starbucks, and Subway Combined . . . and It's Closed on Sundays," *Entrepreneur,* https://www.entrepreneur.com/article/320615.
2. Bryan Cronan, "How Chick-Fil-A's S. Truett Cathy Pioneered the Charitable Business," *Christian Science Monitor,* September 8, 2014, https://www.csmonitor.com/Business/2014/0908/How-Chick-Fil-A-s-S.-Truett-Cathy-pioneered-the-charitable-business.
3. Coleman Wood, "The Original Chicken Sandwich," chick-fil-a.com (blog), May 5, 2017, https://thechickenwire.chick-fil-a.com/inside-chick-fil-a/whats-so-original-about-the-original-chick-fil-a-chicken-sandwich.
4. Matt Forck, "How Navy Captain D. Michael Abrashoff Turned His Ship Around," *Industrial Safety and Hygiene News,* October 31, 2016, https://www.ishn.com/articles/105127-how-navy-captain-d-michael-abrashoff-turned-his-ship-around.

Paradox Five

1. Eric Metaxas, *Seven Women* (Nashville: Thomas Nelson Publishers, 2015), 184.
2. Kathryn Spink, *Mother Teresa: A Complete Authorized Biography* (New York: HarperOne, 2011), 8.
3. Malcolm Muggeridge, *Something Beautiful for God: Mother Teresa of Calcutta* (New York: Harper and Row, 1971), 28.
4. Metaxas, *Seven Women,* 179.
5. https://www.aljazeera.com/news/2020/4/13/who-is-dr-anthony-fauci-the-uss-trusted-voice-on-coronavirus.
6. Tricia McDermott, "A Calm Colonel's Strategic Victory," CBS, cbsnews.com, March 15, 2016, https://www.cbsnews.com/news/a-calm-colonels-strategic-victory/.
7. Daniela Wawra, "Social Intelligence: The Key to Intercultural Communication," *European Journal of English Studies* 13, no. 2 (2009)

163–177, https://www.tandfonline.com/doi/abs/10.1080/13825570902907193?journalCode=neje20.
8. Jonas Sachs, *Winning the Story Wars* (Boston: Harvard Business Review Press, 2012).

Paradox Six

1. Bain and Company, "How Burberry Won Over Millennials," bain.com (blog), December 7, 2015, https://www.bain.com/insights/how-burberry-won-over-millennials/.
2. Bain and Company, "How Burberry Won Over Millennials."
3. Integreat Leadership, " Chick-fil-A Leadercast 2012," integreatleadership.com (blog), https://integreatleadership.com/development/chick-fil-a-leadercast-2012/.
4. Lisa Eadicicco, "Apple's Vision for the Future of TV is Starting to Take Shape—Here's Everything That's New in its Revamped TV App Launching Today," *Business Insider*, May 12, 2019.
5. Bob Thomas, *Walt Disney: An American Original* (Glendale, CA: Disney Editions, 1976), 232.
6. Bradberry and Greaves, *Emotional Intelligence*, 21.
7. Stuart G. Walesh, "Using the Power of Habits to Work Smarter," Helping you Engineer Your Future.com (blog), http://www.helpingyouengineeryourfuture.com/habits-work-smarter.htm.
8. Ichak Adizes, *Managing Corporate Life Cycles* (Carpinteria, CA: The Adizes Institute Publishing, 2004).
9. Gene Hammett, "Jack Welch Always Wanted His Team Members to Take Ownership of Their Work. Here's Why," *Inc.*, August 10, 2018, https://www.inc.com/gene-hammett/3-lessons-from-jack-welch-on-leadership-that-you-dont-learn-in-business-school.html.
10. Andy Crouch, et al, "Leading Beyond the Blizzard: Why Every Organization Is Now a Startup," *Praxis Journal*, March 20, 2020, journal.praxislabs.org/leading-beyond-the-blizzard-why-every-organization-is-now-a-startup-b7f32fb278ff.

Paradox Seven

1. Wills, *Certain Trumpets*, 39.
2. Henry David Thoreau, "Civil Disobedience," in *Walden and Civil Disobedience*, ed. Owen Thomas (New York: W. W. Norton, 1966), 228.
3. Walter Isaacson, *Steve Jobs* (New York: Simon and Schuster, 2011).
4. Amy X. Wang, "No Wonder Young Americans Feel So Important, When Half of Them Finish High School as A Students," *Quartz*, July 19, 2017, https://qz.com/1032183/no-wonder-young-americans-feel-so-important-when-half-of-them-finish-high-school-as-a-students/.
5. Edgar Schein, *Organizational Culture and Leadership* (San Francisco: Wiley and Sons, 2019).

6. Frédérique Autin, Jean-Claude Croizet, "Improving Working Memory Efficiency by Reframing Metacognitive Interpretation of Task Difficulty," *Journal of Experimental Psychology (General)* 141, no. 4 (2012): 610–18, https://pubmed.ncbi.nlm.nih.gov/22390266/.
7. Junchol Park and Bita Moghaddam, "Impact of Anxiety on Prefrontal Cortex Encoding of Cognitive Flexibility," *Neuroscience* 345 (March 2017): 193–202, https://www.ncbi.nlm.nih.gov/pmc/articles/PMC5159328/.
8. https://secure.edweek.org/media/fo-motivation-resources.pdf.

Paradox Eight

1. Neal Gabler, *Walt Disney: The Triumph of the American Imagination* (New York: Vintage Books, 2006), 151–52.
2. Wikipedia contributors, "Epcot," Wikipedia, The Free Encyclopedia, https://en.wikipedia.org/w/index.php?title=Epcot&oldid=1001309734 (accessed January 25, 2021).
3. Gabler, *Walt Disney*, 498.
4. Gabler, *Walt Disney* 571.
5. Gabler, *Walt Disney*, 566–67.
6. Kevin Kelly, *The Inevitable: Understanding the 12 Technological Forces That Will Shape Our Future* (New York: Penguin Books, 2016).

A New Kind of Leader

1. Wikipedia contributors, "Milton Friedman," Wikipedia, The Free Encyclopedia, https://en.wikipedia.org/w/index.php?title=Milton_Friedman&oldid=1000905858 (accessed January 25, 2021).
2. James P. Carse, *Finite and Infinite Games* (New York: Ballantine Books, 1987).
3. Pat Lencioni, "Where CEO's Go Astray," *Journal of Employee Communication*, Table Group, 2001.

INDEX

ABOUT THE AUTHOR

Dr. Tim Elmore is founder and CEO of Growing Leaders (www.growingleaders.com), an Atlanta-based nonprofit organization created to develop emerging leaders. Since founding Growing Leaders in 2003, Elmore has spoken to more than five hundred thousand leaders in businesses, universities, athletic teams, and nonprofit organizations, including The Home Depot, Coca-Cola Bottling Company Consolidated, American Eagle, and Chick-fil-A, as well as the San Francisco Giants, Tampa Bay Buccaneers, and Ohio State University, Stanford University, and the University of Alabama athletics.

His work grew out of twenty years serving alongside Dr. John C. Maxwell, where he focused on leadership for emerging generations. Elmore has appeared in the *Wall Street Journal*, the *Washington Post*, *USA Today*, and *Psychology Today*, and he's been featured on CNN's Headline News and *Fox and Friends* to talk about leading multiple generations in the marketplace. Tim has written more than thirty-five books, including the bestselling *Habitudes: Images That Form Leadership Habits and Attitudes*. Tim and his wife, Pam, have two adult children, Bethany and Jonathan. He and Pam live outside of Atlanta. You can also find his work at TimElmore.com.